WILDLIFE
911

On Patrol

#099

John Borkovich

Arbutus Press
Traverse City, Michigan

Wildlife 911: On Patrol © 2017 John Borkovich
ISBN 978-1-933926-06-3
cover design: Kira Benke kirabenke.designs@gmail.com
www.wildlife911officer.com
editing: Chelsea Borkovich
research: Luke Borkovich

Arbutus Press
Traverse City, Michigan
editor@arbutuspress.com
www.Arbutuspress.com
facebook.com/Arbutuspress

Library of Congress Cataloging-in-Publication Data

Names: Borkovich, John, author.
Title: Wildlife 911 : on patrol / John Borkovich.
Description: Traverse City, Michigan : Arbutus Press, [2017] | Series: Wildlife 911
Identifiers: LCCN 2017015212 | ISBN 9781933926063 (pbk.)
Subjects: LCSH: Wildlife conservation--Law and legislation--United States. |
    Endangered species--Law and legislation--United States. | Poaching--Law
    and legislation--United States.
Classification: LCC KF5640 .B67 2017 | DDC 363.28 [B] --dc23
LC record available at https://lccn.loc.gov/2017015212

Dedication

To my father Walt Borkovich, my mother Allison Borkovich, and my wife Nancy, daughter Chelsea, and son Luke. I am forever proud and forever grateful. I love you.

I give my sincere appreciation and respect to our law enforcement officers, military members, and all of our first responders. It is because of these heroes that we are able to be free and safe to enjoy the beautiful wonders of the natural world.

Memory eternal for all of our fallen law enforcement officers, members of the military and first responders who gave the ultimate sacrifice on our behalf.

Introduction

Wildlife 911 is a compilation of actual incidents that I experienced while I worked as a Michigan Conservation Officer. While on patrol, I met so many great people as they interacted with our natural resources. Most people who hunt, fish, trap, or just enjoy the outdoors are outstanding individuals. However, as in any group, there are always a few bad apples. The stories written about in this book only relate to those who willingly, intentionally, and purposefully chose to break the law.

I have arrested people poaching just about every bird, fish, and animal in America. I have been involved in many serious and dangerous situations. I have had many foot chases and car chases. I have arrested people for everything from murder to arson, and have arrested a terrorist. I was even hit by lightning while working to protect our natural resources.

As outrageous as some of the stories seem, they all actually happened. Readers of this book will feel as if they are doing a "ride along" patrol as we navigate through countless serious and interesting aspects of protecting our natural resources.

So, let's begin our patrol. Get into my patrol truck, snap your seat belt on and get ready to experience many crazy incidents.

Let's check into service now. "9-134 and his readers are in service."

Jimmy Hoffa Bird

What shapes an officer's personality and molds his or her thinking when it comes to dealing with the public? It is certain individual contacts with the public that leaves lasting impressions on an officer's judgment. The old man in this story was one of the people who helped shape my thinking for the rest of my career.

I was just a rookie officer that August day in 1986 when I responded to a complaint that a subject had shot a Great Blue Heron. As I pulled into the driveway of the neatly kept brick ranch home, I could see a well cared for pond and a neatly mowed area surrounding it.

I walked up to the front door, and a very polite old man answered my knock. I smiled and said that I was there regarding an incident which had taken place on his property. The polite man invited me in, and we sat down at his kitchen table. We talked for several minutes as I softened up my suspect and prepared for my upcoming interview.

I eased into my interrogation, and each time I asked an incriminating question, I got an incriminating answer. I then advised the suspect of his Miranda Rights (you know, the right to remain silent, have a lawyer present, and all that), and he easily agreed to speak with me. Now I was on a roll. I asked the suspect a series of questions: were you home today? Did you see a heron on your pond? Do you own a gun? Each question was answered by responses like, "yes I sure did," and "oh yes." I was quite proud of my interview skills, especially for being a new officer. I reveled in my talent of being able to school the man and to get him to confess quickly. I confidently stated to the old man, OK you saw a heron on your pond, you own a shotgun, and you were mad at the heron for eating your fish.

Then I asked him, "Did you shoot the heron?" "Yes I did," was the man's answer. "Alright, tell me what happened" I replied. He said that "the stupid fish eating bird comes every day and eats all my fish, so I shot him." Now

5

I'm thinking, I just solved the case. Not so fast, though, I soon found out who was really getting schooled, and it was me.

I asked to see the dead bird and a smile came to the old man's face. "You're never going to find Jimmy Hoffa, (the UAW teamster boss), and you're never going to find that heron." The rookie officer was now not so confident. The old man was having fun with me. He told me that the Native Americans would call herons "fishing long legs" because they would clean out a fish pond like a vacuum cleans the carpet. I had everything I needed for my case, except for the bird's body.

Then I made some decisions, which molded my way of thinking for the rest of my career. The man was 86 years old. The bird was eating his fish. The man was very cooperative, and he had paid his dues in life. He was a WWII veteran. He paid his taxes, and he took good care of his home and family. The totality of the circumstances made me realize that even though I probably would have won this case in court, there was not much to gain by seeking criminal charges. I smiled and shook the old man's hand and thanked him for being so honest; then I told him not to shoot any more herons. Then I left his house. The old man died the next year and took the heron's secret hiding place to the grave with him.

Poacher Kills a 14-point Buck

S ome people are believable and convincing at face value. Some
people are smooth and good at deception. Some people use
misleading information and lies to avoid getting caught. Some
people plan crimes well in advance. And some criminals never get caught
due to their smooth or slick personality. Some people never get caught
because they use deceptive props or by planting false evidence. This story
involves a subject who was very creative and deceptive and polite and
friendly and who used props and false evidence but who did NOT get away
with the crime.

It was Thanksgiving morning 2003, and my deputized volunteer
conservation officer partner Dave Houser and I began our patrol at 5:00 a.m.
As we patrolled St. Clair County's back roads, we checked several hunters
and saw a few harvested deer.

One of the areas we worked was near the Detroit Edison Greenwood
Energy Center in Avoca. The plant owned six square miles (3,600 acres) of
woods and farmland that was closed to all hunting. Being sort of a refuge,
the property earned a reputation as a place to see big bucks. The big bucks,
in turn, became a magnet for trespassers and poachers. Along the east side of
the Edison property at about 9:30 a.m., we noticed two hunters standing on
the edge of the road. As I pulled up to them, the one hunter said "Hi, John. I
wounded a huge buck on my land adjacent to the energy center's property."
The hunter explained that the deer had run across the road and into the
private property of Detroit Edison. The hunter said he and his son tracked
the deer, found it and then gutted it, but decided not to drag the deer out and
to contact me instead. The hunter asked me if I could follow the blood trail
back to the deer and help them retrieve the buck. After all, they did not want
the deer to go to waste or anything. Being the nice, humane, and cooperative
officer that I was, I agreed to walk with the hunters, without their weapons,

This is the trophy 14-point buck killed by a "creative" poacher.

onto the Edison property to follow the blood trail and to retrieve the deer. So the tracking began, without the need of much tracking expertise or the use of Bloodhound. We were able to follow the visible blood trail about one-third of a mile to the dead 14-point buck. The majestic trophy animal lay gutted already and had a 12 gauge slug hole through both lungs.

From years of experience, I noted to myself that a deer double lunged usually does not run one-third of a mile. The one subject asked me if the buck made the record book. I assured him that indeed it was a book buck. The subjects were a little nervous, but I still shook their hands, congratulated them, and helped drag their trophy out of the woods.

Always asking questions, I began to doubt some of the answers I was getting from the hunters about the incident. Most lung shot deer will "spray" blood out one or both sides of the deer as they run. This particular blood trail showed no signs of a lung shot deer except for the color of the blood. During the hour that I had spent trailing, dragging, and congratulating the hunters, I formulated my opinion that the deer was killed suspiciously. I checked the deer's pupils for the time of death estimation, checked the core body temperature and although leery of the kill, both tests verified the deer was killed that morning, so a nighttime kill was ruled out. As I continued to congratulate (and probe for answers) we were joined by ten or twelve other hunters who had stopped to gawk and to admire the big buck, now lying along the side of the road.

While the other hunters and a St. Clair County Sheriff Deputy were looking at the deer, I asked the hunters to walk with me to the location the buck was shot. I found a shell casing and a blood trail that led from near the hunter's blind all the way across the gravel road. The road was a hard packed, smooth gravel road. Looking at the blood on the road, I noticed the clue that I had been looking for. The blood was in large drops spaced every three or four feet across the road. I asked a series of eight questions (fast, without giving the hunters time to think).

What time did you shoot the deer? Was the deer alone? Was he facing left or right? Did he jump when you shot? Did the deer run fast? Could you see him all the way to the road? Did he run across the road or walk? And did he run real fast? The answers were "8:05 a.m., deer was alone, facing left, jumped when hit, ran fast, saw him all the way across the road, ran real fast". When the hunter gave the excited utterance type answers, he made the mistake of telling me the deer ran real fast across the road.

I put my hand on the now suspect's shoulder and said, "OK, I am not mad at you for lying to me, but you and I need to have a man to man talk." I explained that when a bleeding deer is running, the blood drops in a forward

9

indicating direction, and is not dropped straight down.

This blood was dropped or spilled straight down indicating little or no forward motion. Also, the buck was shot through both lungs and though it was a tough old buck, I doubt it could have run over one-third of a mile before falling. Then I told him that I very much respect the fact that his son (the other hunter) was a United States Marine and because of his service and commitment, I would not include him in the case, as long as he and I could talk through the incident.

The hunter said, "Thank you, officer, for not arresting my son, and here is what really happened." I trespassed on the Detroit Edison Greenwood Plant property and shot the 14-point buck. I then gutted the buck and filled up a 16-ounce plastic Mountain Dew bottle with blood from the deer's heart and lung area. Then I made a false blood trail right back to my blind on our property." Wow, I thought as I tried not to smile with pride. It is simply amazing to realize the lengths people will go to poach, trespass, or harm our resources. I was very proud of myself for being able to figure out what happened on this case. The suspect was then arrested and the Thanksgiving patrol continued.

Exactly one year later on Thanksgiving morning, my VCO Dave Houser and I were driving north past the same hunter's blind who killed the fourteen point buck one year earlier. All of a sudden on our handheld walkie talkie radio we heard, "There he is, I will break his arms if he comes here this year." I turned the patrol car around and I heard very clearly a voice I recognized that belonged to the poacher from one year earlier. "He's turning around right in front of me, that SOB is stopped now and is looking at me." Through the lens of my spotting scope, I could see the hunter talking on a radio and looking at me. I radioed for backup. When a Michigan State Police car and a St. Clair County Sheriff Deputy car pulled up next to my unit, the hunter said, "What do they want? Now the sheriff and state police are here too."

As we began our dangerous walk up to the threatening suspect, we heard him say, "Oh great, they are walking toward my blind now." When I got below the elevated blind, I climbed the suspect's ladder and ordered him out. The suspect came out of his blind and did confess to making the statements on the radio about me. Then he stated that he was just showing off.

The suspect apologized and said that I had treated him fairly the year before and he did not mean any harm by his stupid comments. Enforcement action was taken, and the Thanksgiving deer patrol continued.

Going to Kill American Boys

The following incident happened only one year after the horrific tragedy of the 9/11 terrorist attack on the World Trade Center. Tensions were running high. I am sure that many more people reading this story would side with a proud American law enforcement officer's attitude than would side with extremists with anti-American views.

Too often, we gloss over information or facts so as not to offend anyone. Too darn bad if the truth hurts or offends someone. So let me be blunt and not try to hide any of my feelings or the facts about this case. Yes, the men were foreign. Yes, they were extremists! Yes, they were anti-American!

On several occasions and incidents written about in this book, I mention of making the right decisions when dealing with suspects. Making the correct and proper decision has profound meaning to me.

Officers must always try to make correct decisions. The right decision goes way back when trying to decide to stop or contact someone. The proper decision relates to the area of officer discretion; when to arrest someone and when not to. The correct decision applies to an officer who is not ignoring laws, rules, or policies while working. The right decision is also affected by an officer's respect for humanity. The correct decision is even weighted by an officer's belief in God (religion), meaning that an officer needs to make the proper decision even when no one is watching. Religious beliefs teach us to care for and treat others fairly or humanely. So for lots of reasons I did not shoot these two misguided men.

These subjects were salmon fishing. Michigan Conservation Officers could write an entire book related to salmon snagging and salmon poaching. Some people resort to any means necessary to be able to get a three-foot-long fish. Some people use spearing, shooting, snagging, or any other way possible to get a salmon. These fish are usually very vulnerable while in shallow water.

While patrolling for salmon poachers one night, I spent several hours searching for vehicles parked near a river or stream which I knew contained salmon. These fish are very easy to get, and many times fish poachers would park their cars, run to the creek to spear or snag a salmon, and run away. This type of hit and run activity made it easier to get away without getting caught.

I drove, and I drove, then I spotted a vehicle parked near a river. Yes, the telltale signs were inside the vehicle. A cooler, shoes, an empty wader box, and fishing gear were visible inside the vehicle. I began walking the river bank searching for the fisherman. After about an hour, I heard voices ahead of me. Now about 1:30 a.m., I slowly closed the distance and soon I could see two males fishing along the river's edge. I crawled to a vantage point where I could observe the fishermen and make sure they were not snagging the salmon in front of them.

Then I saw one of the subjects throw a beer bottle into OUR river. I got mad and knew I was going to make an arrest. I crept closer to the suspects and soon I was six feet away, right above them. I was laying on the edge of the bank looking down at them when I got a big surprise. They both pulled out 20-inch long ninja style knives and started stabbing the sandy river bank right below me.

Each man would yell in broken English such comments as, kill the Americans, and I'm going to kill the American boys, as they violently stabbed the bank. I laid there undetected as they threw more beer bottles into the river and cursed and cussed about killing Americans and repeatedly stabbed the sandy bank. "Kill the Americans! Can't wait to see the look on their faces when we stab them," they repeatedly yelled out. Remember, it had only been one year since the horrific events of the September 11th terrorist attack. Someone with so much hatred and disdain for Americans and who possessed such large knives posed a bit of a tactical problem. Police officers are trained that the safe reactionary distance when dealing with an assailant with a knife is 21 feet. So here I was, only six feet away from them, and I knew it was going to be a fun, yet dangerous encounter. I almost laughed to myself as I thought about how these idiots hate the American boys so much and want to kill the American boy because I had a surprise for them. The next time they set their knives down, they were going to meet the American boy.

As they set their knives down, I jumped down at them while displaying my .40 caliber Sig Sauer Model 226 semi-automatic handgun. Several verbal commands and a brief scuffle ensued. The two men were startled and shocked as I aimed my gun at them and loudly gave commands. They thought they were all alone and way back in the woods along the river and here I was, their enemy. Both anti-Americans found themselves face down and placed in American made Smith and Wesson handcuffs. I arrested the suspects and later called the United States Department of Homeland Security and gave them the suspects' information.

Police officers must make snap decisions and must always do the right thing. We are often placed in dangerous and complicated situations and are forced to make correct and fair decisions while still maintaining our personal safety. This situation and outcome were completely in my hands. There were no witnesses, we were over one mile from any road, there were two possible terrorists, and it was in the middle of the night. I thought about shooting them both. But, I decided to act properly, ethically, and safely and just arrest them.

Again, police officers are held to a higher standard and have a huge responsibility placed on them while dealing with the public.

Another unusual situation, another dangerous close call that I handled safely and properly I thought to myself, smiling as I drove home that night.

Objects in Mirror are Closer Than They Appear

In life, things are not always as they appear. Just look at your car or truck's side view mirror. The writing on the mirror says, "objects in mirror are closer than they appear." Smoke and mirrors also disguise a lot of things. Magicians and criminals can be real good at deception and changing the looks of certain things. Some crime scenes take awhile to analyze and figure out. This particular scene looked so innocent and normal at first. It was just a van stuck on the shoulder of the road.

One late night deer patrol, I had Mark Johnson, a dispatcher for St. Clair County Sheriff Department, working with me. We rode along hunting for violators, as we told deer, fish, baseball, and family stories. Up ahead on the gravel road, we noticed a vehicle stuck on the shoulder of the road. Two subjects were pushing the van, and the other was trying to drive the van out of the snow bank. Not budging, Mark and I got out to help push the van. While we were in the snow bank and pushing, I noticed something peculiar. There was a deer trapped under the subjects' van. That's odd, we thought, the three guys from the van never mentioned having been involved in a car-deer accident.

To our amazement, the young deer was still alive. Now with renewed energy and determination, we pushed on the van again. This time, we were able to move the vehicle about six feet, and surprise, the yearling doe that was trapped under the van jumped up and ran into the woods to the south. Great news and a happy ending, for the deer that is. So I said, have a good night, and we drove away. NOT!

Suspicious of why none of the subjects mentioned hitting the deer, we began checking a little closer. The stuck subjects smelled like alcohol, and one of the men had 12 gauge shotgun slugs in his pocket. Hmmm, we became even more suspicious of the subjects. A consent search of the van revealed more shotgun slugs, a plugged in spotlight, a hunting knife, and a couple of open beers. But we found no gun. One of the subjects was more nervous than the other two, so I zeroed in on him. He was very inconsistent with his answers about how the deer got under the van and why they had shotgun slugs and a spotlight with them. The subject inadvertently glanced down the road a couple of times. Finally, we looked down the road a bit and found fresh boot tracks. The tracks led us right to a loaded 12-gauge shotgun hidden behind a large Oak tree. It was loaded with the same Remington brand slugs that were in the van and in subject's pocket. The jig was up.

They gave us written confessions that they were shining and shooting at some deer in the field and when the deer tried running across the road towards the woods, they accelerated in reverse to run the deer down. That's when they hit the small doe which got stuck under the van and caused them to go into the ditch. The driver should have used his side view mirror. I think in the small print it would have said, "Objects in mirror are closer than you think to putting you in jail." They then hid their gun in the woods in case anyone showed up.

They almost got away with their poaching and bad behavior except for one detail. The very animal that they were shooting at and trying to run over got revenge by being trapped underneath their vehicle. Paybacks are sweet sometimes.

Eagle Eye

One time I found a dead Bald Eagle. It was a very old, mature bird. Staring at the bird, I almost teared up. The sadness of losing such an icon, which was part of our history, really hit me hard. The bird that the Native American Indians respected, cherished, and worshiped, the bird that is the symbol of freedom, was lying there dead in front of me.

Looking at the eagle was a very solemn and sobering experience. Such a great hunter, gifted by God with ultimate eyesight, lay on the ground, succumbed to death and (like all of us) proved to be mortal. I stared at the mighty bird and wondered what it had seen during its lifetime. If only it could talk and tell us what beauty and interesting aspects of nature it saw during the 20 or 30 years that it flew above us.

I checked the area and the bird and found no signs of foul play or poaching. The eagle died close to its nest, so I assumed it died of old age.

The other reason that I felt so close to the eagle was the fact that like eagles, I am also blessed with exceptional eyesight. At one of my eye exams, the ophthalmologist called me Chuck Yeager. Chuck Yeager is one of the most famous fighter pilots of all time. He was a United States Air Force Brigadier General. The doctor explained the Chuck Yeager story to me. Evidently, Chuck Yeager's exceptional vision aided him in spotting enemy aircraft and allowed him to do amazing things with his aircraft. As my eye exam continued, the ophthalmologist kept making reference to my eyesight and could not believe how well that I could see.

Like the eagle's eyesight and like the fighter pilot's eyesight, my enhanced eyesight allowed me to see so much while I hunted. I used my eyesight to my advantage for years while working to protect our natural resources. But unlike eagles, I can convey the sights that I saw over the years.

I Think I Know Who You Are

Law enforcement officers need to be "at the ready" at all times. So often in police work, an officer goes from mundane, slow, and almost boring periods of time to exciting, explosive, and heart pounding action. Somehow everything changes in the blink of an eye. It takes a special person to be able to flip a switch (on demand) to go from no action to intense action. All at once, this roller coaster of emotion is what makes this job so interesting to us. When things happen or go bad, there is no time for hesitation, no time for indecision, and no time to rely on others. Slow reactions, poor decision making, or freezing up can also put an officer's safety in jeopardy. Quick thinking, quick reacting officers fair much better than indecisive officers when engaged with suspects.

It is somehow very enjoyable to be placed in situations where one goes from zero to 60 in just 2.1 seconds. I can compare the experience to what it feels like to sit in a roller coaster as the car is moving slowly up the track. Click, click, click, then when the car reaches the top, it is suddenly in a freefall. This swing of emotion happened one day while I was archery deer hunting on a sunny, calm, beautiful October evening.

Although my 40-acre leased hunting land produced some good hunting over the years, hunting there was not always enjoyable. For some reason, the property was like a magnet for trespassers. The trespassing was so bad that I would wear a clean uniform shirt under my camouflage jumpsuit. I would also keep a ticket book in my hunting backpack.

Well, on this particular October evening, I relaxed as I realized that I finally had the woods to myself. The bright red, yellow, and orange leaves around me were in their peak color phase. The sky was bright blue, and I could hear the water from the babbling brook flowing in front of me. Nearby to the east, I watched turkeys and squirrels feasting on Beechnut. The fresh smell of fall and the aroma from the cedar trees around me was simply amazing. This clear, windless fall day reminded me once again of how lucky that I was to be able to enjoy the outdoors, how lucky I was to be able to go hunting and reminded me to thank God that I was alive and well.

As I sat perched in my tree stand over twenty feet off the ground, I marveled at the bird's eye view that I had as the forest came alive. I had prepared all of my hunting gear in anticipation of a good hunt. I had washed all of my clothing with scent-free soap (I used special UV killer soap) and I also sprayed myself from my head to my feet with scent eliminating spray. So here I was, all nestled in and confident that the animals around me did not know that I was in the woods.

I first saw a doe and two fawns walking unalarmed near my location. Then I saw a young three-point buck milling around in front of me. Then I caught a glimpse of movement to my east and saw part of a bone white antler moving through a thicket. A lot of heart pounding and labored breathing hit me (maybe a little buck fever). Soon I saw the healthy eight-point buck emerge from the brush and walk almost directly under my tree stand.

Surveying the scene unfolding beneath me was so wonderful and pristine until all at once, all five of the deer froze and raised their heads. Each one of the deer looked to the southeast. Not just looked, but looked with intent. When a deer senses danger or hears danger, it will look at the suspected area with its ears trained very far forward in an attempt to hear possible approaching danger. All of the deer had their ears in this far forward position signaling to me that something was coming. Was it a dog? Was it a coyote? No worse, it was some idiot trespassing. The trespasser saw the deer near my location and was trying to get closer to them. The errant hunter was now in sneak mode, dressed in full camo and carrying a shotgun! It was not firearm season for almost another month.

The trespasser looked like some Elmer Fudd dude as he walked with his gun shouldered and aimed as he got ready to shoot the deer. I was right, none of the animals knew that I was in the woods hunting. When the poacher got open for a shot, all of the deer bolted and ran to the north. The idiot kept walking toward my location while still aiming his gun. When he was only about 50 yards away from me, he looked at me and immediately started running. I almost forgot that I was way up in a tree, but then I remembered to climb down the tree before I started chasing after the trespasser.

I began running after the trespasser who had just ruined my hunt. I was dressed in full camo and wearing a full facemask and did not have any weapon on me. Real smart, huh?. My fleeing trespasser was also dressed in camo, but the odds were slightly in his favor. He had a shotgun and a head start. I closed the gap and was gaining on the running fool and soon I got close enough to tackle him. Then I tackled him with a little vengeance. I rolled him over and thought about hitting him but decided not to. Then it occurred to me that I had better identify myself and tell him who just ran him down like a dog and was pinning him to the ground. I said, "I suppose I better show you who I am" as I began tearing open my jumpsuit. But before I could expose my uniform shirt, the subject said, "I think I know who you are, John." The poacher actually did know me. We met one time a few years earlier after I arrested him following a high-speed chase. Yes, I caught him after he fled from me in his pickup truck at speeds of over 100 mph and yes I caught him after chasing him on foot while he was running from me.

So, I guess we were actually like old friends by now.

I said, "Then why the bleep did you come here in the first place if you knew who I was?" I was shocked, that someone would pick the very woods that I was hunting in to go poaching. The trespasser told me that he had just bought the Remington Model 870 12 gauge shotgun earlier that same day. He told me that he thought that I would be out working catching poachers instead of hunting. I was so mad at having yet another hunt ruined by a trespasser that I ignored or forgot the fact that I was unarmed and chasing a man with a loaded shotgun with slugs. Oh well, it was worth the risk, and at least I got something when I went hunting that day.

This whole incident exposes how bad the trespass problem really is. I feel sorry for so many other hunters that don't have arrest powers and usually don't chase down and tackle armed trespassers. If the thought of my presence didn't deter this trespasser from coming on my hunting land, then where is the deterrent for trespassers from running wild on everybody's land?

"You Have Your Whole Life To Hunt With Your Dad." Really?

What prepares a person to become a law enforcement officer? What readies an officers' mind and body to withstand the rigors placed upon police when dealing with dangerous situations? Along with an officers' genetic and athletic makeup, there are certain incidents that help shape an officers' mind and body. One such incident happened to me when I was a high school basketball player.

Basketball practice began each year in November. I missed two days of practice, not to go drinking, not to break into houses or to steal cars or to sell drugs, but to go up north deer hunting with my father and my two brothers. After spending two memorable days with my family at deer camp, I got my gym bag ready and headed for basketball practice after school. I felt so amazingly alive inside. I was so rejuvenated from the sights, sounds, and smells of nature that I almost forgot about missing the two practices.

Our team practiced, then ran our four line suicide sprints, shot 25 free throws, then we all headed for the locker room. I heard my coach say, "John, you shouldn't have missed practice, you have your whole life to go hunting with your dad." He then said, "I'm not through with you, John, now get back on the line to run." I began running suicide sprints at 5:30. At 7:30, I was almost dead, but still running! Earlier, I could see some of my friends from the team checking in on me through the gym doors, then after awhile I could not see much of anything anymore. I would run from the end line to the foul line, then back, then to half court, then back, then to the opposite foul line and back, then all the way to the other end line, then back. I did this over and over. My coach stood near me with his arms folded over his chest and he had a silver whistle in his mouth. He would blow that stupid whistle so very loudly when it was time for me to start a new series of sprints.

After awhile, everything got foggy. The smell of the wood gym floor that I always had liked and the exciting sound of basketballs bouncing on the hardwood court now left me. I could no longer hear very well. I could no longer smell. I no longer knew what I was doing. I started seeing stars and having short blackout spells. I could not remember which line that I was supposed to be running to. The next step in my loss of consciousness was when I would run, all wobbly, the full length of the gym floor then crash into the cold block wall at the other end of the gym. "Get up, get up John," is what I faintly heard. Then the silver whistle would blow again. The coach's yelling, and the loud whistle were the only sounds that I could hear. I would get up, stumble, then run all the way down the court and crash into the opposite wall again.

Now after 7:30 p.m., the coach said, "Now go take a shower." Being delirious, my chest heaving and going in and out of consciousness, I somehow made it to the showers.

This poor coach knew nothing about hunting. He never even hunted or fished or participated in outdoor recreation. His ignorance about the value of hunting and the value of hunting with family and friends led him to treat me so poorly. His lack of knowledge about hunting led him to believe that all hunters go hunting just to get drunk or to go poaching. If he would have known more about the sacred feelings that most hunters have in their hearts, then he would not have been so aggressively trying to punish me.

The coach was trying to teach me a lesson, and by being so tough on me, he was planning to gain respect from his athletes for years to come. The only problem was that the player that he tried to break down was an athlete who loved his family and hunting so much that nothing short of killing him with a bullet would break his family and hunting spirit. The future conservation officer who seemed almost like a mutant withstood the cruel and unusual punishment somehow.

Later that night, both my brothers kept getting my parents up to check on me as I screamed aloud from severe leg cramps. They gave me water and salt pills.

The next day at school was terrible. I could hardly walk. All of my friends stared at me like they were looking at a ghost. How and why did I make it through the grueling ordeal?

That evening after practice as I headed toward the locker room, I was thinking about how good it was going to feel to go home and rest my weary body. But then I heard, "John, I'm not through with you yet, you missed two days, and you owe me one more day of sprints, now get on the line." Oh boy, that was a very disheartening thing to hear.

I got on the gym's end line, the silver whistle blew, and the cruel punishment continued. The same insane running and delirious stumbling occurred the second night. But the same outcome came to be again. Him trying to break me but failing to do so!

Nowadays, my family would have won millions of dollars in lawsuit money from the school district from the errant coach's actions.

After the coach had failed in his attempt to break me (or kill me), he had a newfound respect for me. I went on to be a good basketball player and contributed a lot to my team.

Sometimes I think that all high school athletes should go through a similar experience (only toned down a lot). The young athletes would learn just how much the human body and mind can take. I think it would be similar to how Marines, Navy Seals, Army Rangers, and other special forces train their own.

Anyway, I sort of liked my coach. I respected him for his love of basketball. I appreciated his demand for respect. But he was wrong. He obviously did not see or get the big picture in life. Oh how I wish the coach was right about one thing, I so dearly wish I had my whole life to hunt with my dad! I sadly lost my dad in 2011. The coach was wrong about a lot of things, especially his insensitive and thoughtless comment that "You have your whole life to hunt with your dad".

Most people would have either quit or died. I did not do either. What I did do was learn what my limits were. I learned that my mind and body really had no limits. The lessons learned from those horrible days back in high school became etched into my mind, body, and soul for life.

On so many occasions during my career in law enforcement, I needed to reach back to the painful basketball experience for help. I knew that I had the determination, strength, courage, stamina, and willpower to endure and survive any situation that I found myself in.

Caviar Anyone?

Great Lakes sturgeon have been protected for years. The sturgeon population has been declining for decades and protection of these large prehistoric fish, is a statewide priority. Great Lakes sturgeon can live to be 100 years old. Unfortunately, some poachers target the female surgeon just for the fish's eggs. The eggs (caviar) are a delicacy and are regarded as the second most desirable caviar in the world, second only to the White Russian Caviar.

In an attempt to assure stable sturgeon populations for future generations, fish and game officers spend a lot of time patrolling for sturgeon poachers. There are even volunteer sturgeon watch groups who help protect these large fish. These great, caring people volunteer their time to help watch and protect our valuable surgeon resource. They work long hours, day and night, observing areas where sturgeon are spawning and have an enormous impact on the amount of sturgeon poaching. Another group is called St. Clair Detroit River Sturgeon for Tomorrow. This group does a great job educating the public and helping protect sturgeon.

Two of the group's members, Dave Dortman and Michael Thomas are former and current DNR employees who work full time as advocates for sturgeon, and they do a remarkable job. Conservation officers can't be at all places at all times, so the volunteers serve as extra eyes to help spot possible poaching. They call the DNR when they see suspicious activity. The Department of Natural Resources has placed a high priority on protecting our sturgeon. The state even offers a $1,500 reward to a person who turns in a sturgeon poacher. Officers even participate in directed group patrols working hard to protect the "dinosaur looking fish." On many other occasions, officers just go alone on patrol searching for sturgeon poachers.

Most of my sturgeon activity took place at night. However, it is not easy working at night. It is also not easy working extra long hours. It is not easy working out in the elements, being sometimes cold or raining outside. It is not easy giving up relaxing personal time, family time, and regular sleep time. Although not always easy, working late at night is necessary to be able to catch serious sturgeon poachers.

One late night in June, (during the closed season on sturgeon) one of my partners, Dick Sawkin and I were working along the St. Clair River targeting sturgeon poachers. We were hiding in the shadows in a storage area of a marina. We hid near several broken down boats and some junk piles. We could see some fishermen using hefty 10-foot long fishing rods. From the looks of their gear, we knew they were targeting sturgeon in the St. Clair River in front of them.

After a couple of hours, we heard the ding, ding, ding of the bell on one of the subject's large fishing poles. We watched one of the subjects begin reeling in something large. His pole nearly bent in half as the monster fish tried to stay away from the pier the fishermen were on.

My partner and I knew that the big fish was most likely a sturgeon, and the longer the fisherman reeled, the more excited and anxious we became. We knew that if the fishermen were not poachers, that they would just photograph the big fish and then let it go.

So we waited and watched the fishermen reel the fish in (now it had been over 20 minutes since the fish bit). Then another subject used a huge landing net and netted the fish. Sweet, indeed the fish was a sturgeon, and it was big, about six feet long! Then, in a rather surprising move, one subject pushed a yellow rope through the fish's gills. Then they immediately began dragging the huge fish toward their parked van. They pulled the big fish similar to the way hunters would drag a deer out of the woods. These guys were really

The author holds a nearly six-foot long sturgeon killed by poachers.

moving fast, almost running. They were moving so fast that before we could climb out of our hiding spots, the poachers swung the van's side door open and threw the sturgeon inside. Then they jumped in and began speeding away. The big one that got away, I thought as I began sprinting to my patrol truck that was parked at least a hundred yards away.

Being such a dark night helped to conceal us during the surveillance stage, but the darkness almost helped the poachers get away. As I was running as fast as I could, I ran directly into an angle iron sign frame! The bottom chord of the frame was a horizontal piece of angle iron that was about one foot off the ground. WHACK, my shin hit the steel. You know, the shin bone. I went down like I was shot. The pain was great but not as great as my desire to catch up to the maroon van with the poached sturgeon in it.

Soon I was back on my feet and made it to my patrol truck. My eyes were watering from the pain, and I could barely see the taillights of the suspects' van as they sped away westbound. I closed the distance between the good guy and the bad guys, and soon I hit my flashers. The vehicle continued westbound, then I activated my siren and advised dispatch of what was going on. With lights on and my siren blaring, I pulled up closer to the suspects' van. The van then pulled abruptly into an apartment building in a last second effort to ditch me. The passenger door flung open and I accelerated right at it. I jumped out and ordered the suspects to raise their hands, and advised them that they were under arrest. Soon Dick Sawkin along with six K-9 units came wheeling in to back me up. The K-9 cops had just finished training nearby when they heard my call for assistance. I'm not sure who was more shocked, the K-9 police upon seeing the huge fish in the van, or the suspects for being surrounded by six tactical looking K-9 officers. We arrested the poachers and impounded their van.

It was almost daylight when our successful night came to an end. When the fish poachers left in such a hurry in the middle of the night, they left their tackle boxes and fishing rods on the pier. Unbeknownst to us, some early-morning walkers found the fishing gear on the pier with no one around and assumed someone had fallen into the river. Local police and marine officers responded to search for the missing fishermen. One of my partners, Ron Pinson, responded and was able to figure out what had happened. Ron was able to verify that the fishing tackle belonged to the sturgeon poachers and that they had not fallen into the cold water and drowned, but instead, they were in hot water in jail.

Three Gun Cases Only Two Guns

P olice officers must think outside the box sometimes and do some crazy things to catch a poacher. Sometimes an officer even needs to ride in the poacher's truck to catch him. What? Ride with the bad guys? Yes, sometimes. The phrase "all is fair in love, war, and catching poachers" seems to be a fitting one.

Nightfall came quickly on this late November night, and darkness signaled the end of another day of deer hunting. Poacher hunting, unlike deer hunting, did not end at the end of daylight, however. After working to catch poachers all day, I began my night hunting routine of driving around on back roads searching for suspicious activity.

As I searched and searched, I ended up checking near a power plant area. The area had a high concentration of deer and was home to some big bucks. The lure of big bucks often led poachers to gravitate to the area. The road that I was driving on was a dividing line between land closed to hunting and private land that was legally hunted. The land to my left became sort of a refuge because of the no hunting rules.

As I traveled westbound, I began following a slow moving pickup truck. I used my right turn signal and turned into a driveway to let the occupants of the slow roller assume that no one was behind them anymore. Then I hit all of my kill switches which disabled my headlights, brakelights, and tail lights. Now blacked out, I began following the slow truck again, only this time, no one in the truck knew that I was following them. As I was following the truck, the driver brought it to a stop on the gravel road. I watched intently for such things as a spotlight, gun barrels, or possible trespassers being picked up. But there was no activity at all. Then after about one minute, the truck continued westbound with me following behind.

After wandering aimlessly for about eight miles or so, the truck slowly came to a stop in the same exact spot that it had stopped at earlier. I watched with anticipation, but nothing happened again. I deduced that the guys in the truck were driving the "pick up vehicle" for a poacher that they were supposed to meet at that one particular spot. The hiding poacher must have been laying down in the woods and must have seen my patrol truck trailing the pickup vehicle because he did not come out to his friends' truck either time it stopped to pick him up.

The truck left the location again. After letting them get about four miles away, I stopped the truck. The subjects in the red truck stated that they were just driving around after a day of hunting. I checked their guns to make sure that they were not loaded. The first gun case had an unloaded Remington shotgun in it. The second case had an unloaded Mossberg shotgun in it. The third gun case had no gun in it. It was empty. Now my hunch that there was another hiding hunter became more of a possibility. I could smell alcohol coming from inside of the truck. Then I saw a Miller Lite beer can partially hidden under a coat. I grabbed the half-full beer can and I could feel that it was still cold. Both men in the truck admitted that they had been drinking.

I checked the records of the men through my radio LEIN channel. What a surprise, the driver had a prior conviction for drunk driving. Leverage, I thought. I calmly advised the driver that I would make a deal with him. He did not seem drunk yet, but maybe close to it. I told him that I would not pursue alcohol charges on him if he took me back to the designated pick-up spot for the third hunter.

"I can't do that, he is my friend," the driver said. I told him that I could not overlook the open alcohol then. The driver was stuck with no choice. He said that I could follow him to pick up his poaching friend. Oh, not so fast, I thought. I did not want to follow him again; I wanted to ride inside of his vehicle. Kind of an eerie experience it was as I climbed into the cab of the red truck. Sort of funny though, because we laughed together and talked like three old poaching friends would do as we drove up to the prearranged spot. The driver slowly came to a stop for the third time at the secret spot. After about 10 seconds, a figure in the dark carrying a gun came running up to my side door. I smiled to myself, knowing that my plan was working. The poacher, dressed in full camo, ran up to the truck and hurriedly opened the door next to me. His "safety at last" feeling must have come to an abrupt ending when he went to jump into the truck and found me sitting in his seat. The very person he was hiding from was in his friends' truck and now grabbing his scoped gun. Startled and dumbfounded, the man froze up and just stood there as I arrested him.

We all laughed aloud at the unfolding scene. Can you imagine the shock the poacher must have felt deep down inside when he found the enemy was inside of the getaway vehicle? As I said, all is fair in love, war, and hunting poachers.

27

Dead Hawks, Owls, Ducks, and a Human Skull

Thisbook is not about religion. It is not writings that encourage or choose one religion over another. These stories are not meant to disparage or discount other people's beliefs or values.

But some people do strange things and have odd ways of worshipping. So odd that I shake my head in disbelief when I recall my contact with these strange worshippers.

In America, everyone has the right to practice their religion and have their own beliefs. That is one of the great foundations of the U. S. Constitution. We do not have a state-run religion, and we are not some communist run country where a dictator tells us how to think or how to worship and what to believe. Even though freedom and freedom of religion is a good thing, it's also permissible and our right to be shocked or think other people are strange for the way they worship, pray, or act. This case shocked me, and yes, I think the suspects were strange.

Being experts at anything to do with the outdoors, Michigan Conservation Officers are often asked to assist other police agencies when they get involved in fish and wildlife cases. One such call for backup came from the Port Huron Police Department on a sunny fall afternoon.

Port Huron Police Officers needed my help when they found several dead ducks on the porch of a home in Port Huron. I arrived on location, two city officers met me and showed me the ducks. It was duck season after all, and I figured that we would just ask the homeowner about the ducks and inquire if he had been duck hunting. A very straightforward plan we reasoned. But the plan took a strange twist when an enormous male subject wearing all black clothing answered the door. The man was very polite and cooperative, but when I asked him about the ducks, things began getting creepy. The homeowner told me that the ducks were part of his satanic worship. My PHPD partners were looking at me with confusion as I said,

"Oh sure, that's really cool, do you have more birds or animals you worship?" "Sure, lots of them" answered the subject. "Oh that's really neat," I said. "Can we see the worship site?" "Uh, I guess," said the subject. I had the homeowner sign a form stating that he was giving us permission to search his home for more wildlife.

A consent search is an exception to the 4th Amendment right against illegal searches, so in we went.

Having the legal right to enter the subject's home and having a cooperative homeowner made our original entry seem routine, at least to me, not so much for my city officer friends. As we walked down the basement stairs, we were greeted by two other subjects dressed in all black. I could see my partners walking in the alert position with their hands near their holstered weapons. When we reached the bottom of the stairs, we could barely see; the basement window well panes were painted all black, and the only lights on were blacklights! Hanging from the ceiling were all sorts of dead birds and animals; skulls, skeletons, feathers, feet, and claws were suspended with monofilament fishing line. Several were hanging over the occupants' beds and pillows. As we walked around in amazement, I began making mental notes of wildlife violations, all the while looking for more as I acted interested in their strangeness. There's an owl skull, there's a Red-tailed Hawk, there's an eagle claw I thought as we kept our tour going. At the far end of the basement, we could see several large candles burning. As we approached the candles, we noticed a marble stand with a human skull on it. Grave robbing was another crime to add to our list, I thought. We continued searching and began to wonder what was going on in this place. Very calmly, the homeowner explained that the human skull was part of their temple of worship, complete with all sorts of burning candles and incense. Wow, now my right hand was on my holstered handgun. There were glass shelves full of dead animals and animal parts. Being already shocked, weirded out, and on edge, we continued walking around the basement still very dark, full of incense smoke and very creepy. When a hanging sheet (used for a door) began moving, we prepared for action. What's next, we thought? Then a 4-foot 7-inch tall very old hunched back lady came out from the room and shuffled past us. Then, the homeowner said, "Oh that's granny, we let her live here for free until she dies" (she did have a nice skull, we thought). Oh my, this place was starting to get to us. We finally, turned on all the lights and tabulated the violations and issued the subjects tickets for possession of illegal wildlife and possession of a human skull. The Port Huron officers and I were very glad to leave this home intact.

Deer Shining While Riding on Trunk

Ever see a mirage? You know, when you are driving down the road on a hot summer day, and you see water or a shiny spot on the road ahead of you. Believe me, I thought I was seeing a mirage one night as I snuck up behind a vehicle that was shining for deer.

Up ahead of me about two miles away, I could see a bright spotlight bouncing across the sky. Deer shiners, my target, I locked on the light like a GPS guided missile locks on a target. Soon I had a visual on the suspect's vehicle. It was a dark and drizzly night, and I was driving while blacked out. Driving without my headlights usually gave me the element of surprise. I would zoom up on the poaching suspect's vehicle then when I got real close, I would hit the flashers and use the surprise shock-factor to my benefit. This time I was the one who got surprised.

When I got real close to the shining vehicle, I lit them up. From only 20 feet away, I was looking at two men riding on the trunk of the car. One was holding a gun, and the other was holding a spotlight. Their friend would drive them around and they would shine and shoot at deer. Expecting the poachers to be inside of their vehicle where I could usually contain them, I was shocked to see them on the trunk. The car stopped, and in a pre-planned move both men sitting on the truck immediately jumped off the vehicle and rolled onto the road. Both men took off running. I tackled one of the poachers and handcuffed him and then took the driver into custody. The third poacher ran into a 200-acre standing corn field in total darkness. I knew in baseball, two for three is a real good average, but I wanted to catch 100% of my poachers. I ran into the corn maze for 15 minutes, then returned to check on my handcuffed buddies. Backup cars soon arrived. I walked and walked for hours searching the eight-foot tall corn field for my running poacher who was still carrying a gun. Eventually, frustrated and angry, I returned to the scene where I stopped the vehicle. After spending hours trying to identify the third poacher, I got his name and soon had his address. It was not until the next morning that the fleeing violator made it back to his house, only about 10 miles away. I met him and we had a cordial conversation and he gave me a written confession as to his role in the deer poaching.

I found out that the plan was to ride outside on the trunk so they could run off if they saw any officers. Nice plan, nice try. They lost.

P.S. Oh, by the way, I arrested the same (runner) subject two years later for three illegal deer and four years later for shining with a scoped gun- only this time he was sitting in the warm cab of his truck. Slow learner, but he did learn to stay inside the comfort of the warm truck.

Dragging my Dad

Rumor has it that I am a tough guy. Quite rough, quite hard, quite wild, a totally bad dude. I guess at times I was. But most of the time, the, vast majority of the time, I was just a nice guy who gave too many warnings and shook lots of hands and treated people well. One time, though, I vividly remember deviating from my nice-guy routine. No more kind and gentle approach when things went bad on this case.

In early October, I was patrolling with my father, Walter Borkovich, a State of Michigan Volunteer Conservation Officer. We noticed two subjects shooting into Mill Creek with a .22 caliber semi-automatic scoped rifle. Well, knowing that most squirrels don't live under water, we assumed that they were shooting at fish. I dropped my dad off who was wearing plain clothes and had him walk up to witness what the subjects were shooting at. Bang! They shot another salmon right in front of my dad.

The subjects told my dad that if the DNR comes, they will shoot and kill him. As they were talking, one of them said, "You're not the DNR are you?" As I was watching with binoculars from my hiding spot, I saw one of them reach over and feel the bulletproof vest under the jacket my father was wearing. Seeing this, I ran back to my patrol car and began driving up to the suspects. The subjects jumped into their car, and as my dad reached into the vehicle to take the keys out of the ignition, the driver began backing up while dragging my dad. THE POACHERS WERE DRAGGING MY DAD!
I pulled up and ran toward the vehicle and dove at the driver. He had his left hand on the steering wheel while holding a 16-ounce Budweiser in the same hand. I violently hit the driver's arm to break every bone in his body, forcing him to release his grip. The beer sprayed everywhere. I grabbed the driver, placed the vehicle in park, then pulled the disgusting, useless, pathetic, sickening, deplorable poacher from the vehicle. It was very tempting to manhandle the suspect because he had almost injured or killed my best friend, my father. I refrained and kept my composure, and arrested the suspects without further incident.

A Shotgun and a J Plug

Berle Ives was a legendary storyteller. O.J. Simpson was a great liar. A lot of politicians are real good at not telling the truth. Bernie Madoff was a scam artist. Storytelling, lying, hiding the truth, and deception are just a few of the tools poachers use in their attempt to break the law. Law enforcement officers have heard all the excuses. Many violators get away with their crimes because they are very good liars or possess the poker face trait. Many other poachers get away with their crime through the use of props and false information. Sometimes, us officers see through the lies and props.

Another beautiful October day found me driving the back roads near a portion of the Black River. I had spotted five salmon swimming around in a gravel shoal in the river earlier in the day. So, I hid my patrol car and found a hiding spot so I could sort of babysit the spawning fish. Soon, a vehicle pulled up near the river, and two subjects gathered their tackle and headed down to the river. Their tackle is what got my attention. One subject was carrying a short snagging style rod with a large J plug lure attached to his 60-pound test line. For someone who trolls the Great Lakes, a J-plug would be a normal type of lure, but on this spot, where the river was only 2 feet deep, I had to wonder what he was doing. What made me even more suspicious was that the other subject was carrying a 12 gauge single shot shotgun. I decided that the two subjects were worth following as they began their walk along the river. Sure enough, only minutes later, the subject with the shotgun raised his gun and shot a 20-pound salmon right in its side.

I watched as the other subject with the snagging rod ran to the river and grabbed the salmon. As the poachers looked all around for me, they set their plan in motion. The subject with the fishing rod hooked the J plug into the mouth of the fish and then cut his line about 1 foot from the salmon's mouth. The other subject put the fish in his large landing net and the stumblebums started walking out toward their vehicle. I came out of my hiding spot and contacted the fishermen. Before I could say a word, the subjects began telling me their prearranged story.

One subject went on to say that he was fishing with his J plug and knew that salmon love big lures like his. He said he reeled in this large salmon, but then just as his friend was going to net the fish, his line broke. Luckily it fell into the net. "See, here is the proof, the lure is still in his mouth," he said. I thought to myself not a bad plan (fable) except for one big detail. The big detail they forgot about was the 12 gauge slug hole in the side of the salmon. The subjects told me that someone else must have shot the fish right before it bit on their great lure that they were using.

I then told them that I saw the whole thing and that I was amused at their creative story.

I wonder if these two knuckleheads were as creative in their high school English writing class. I issued tickets for the illegal killing and possession of the salmon.

Searching for Lost Hunter

Police officers get put in the position of being sued due to the nature of our work and our position of authority. By driving fast, going hands-on with criminals, and the use or threat of deadly force, we face a higher risk of being sued than the general public does.

Police often find themselves in situations and locations where the U.S. Constitution provides protection to citizens. Through the many high-speed chases, foot chases, armed robbery arrests, open field tackles and take-downs, physical contacts, outright fights, searches and search warrants, armed stand-offs, and thousands of arrests, I have never been sued. But one occasion, where I am sure I could have been sued when all I was doing was trying to find a missing hunter.

On November 15th, the first day of the firearm deer season, I drove up to three hunters who were heading out to hunt in the Port Huron State Game Area. It was about 2:30 p.m. when I wished the three hunters luck, then I kept patrolling. About five hours later, and now being pitch dark, I drove up to the same hunters vehicle where I was met by only two of the hunters. The two hunters were visibly shaken and stated that they could not find the other hunter named Joe. They advised me that Joe was hunting back in the woods past the field, but feared that Joe was either lost, badly hurt, or worse.

I used my spotlight, siren, and loudspeaker to try to give the lost hunter guidance back to his vehicle. But no Joe. After a while, and with still no sign of Joe, I decided to drive through the tall grass field which was about 40 acres in size. I used my spotlight to search the area and used my loudspeaker to call out to Joe dozens and dozens of times. I drove through the field towards the woods where Joe was hunting. All of a sudden, I had a divine intervention, and I slammed on the brakes. What, I thought, if the lost hunter was not in the woods and was actually in the tall grass field instead. I stopped the truck and got out of the truck to yell for Joe. As I walked around in front of my truck, I saw Joe. He was under my truck!!! The lost hunter was laying under my truck. Only Joe's waist and legs were sticking out, and his upper body was under my vehicle. I used my flashlight, afraid to see what I might see, to check under my truck. Joe's head was only eight inches in front of my right front tire. I felt sick. Oh my God. Why did this have to happen? I ran over Joe.

The fool hunter had gotten drunk and had passed out next to his shotgun, Gin, and beer bottles. Once I recognized that Joe was not run over or dead, I pulled his sorry drunk butt out from under my patrol truck and gently placed him under arrest.

I was very mad and shook up because of what almost happened. Here I was trying to help another human being. But instead of being credited for being helpful, the newspaper front page headline would have read "Conservation officer drives over and kills innocent deer hunter while the hunter was just taking a nap." The lawsuit and negative publicity would have been unbearable for an officer who was, through care and compassion, trying to find a lost hunter. Wow, I give thanks for the help I got that made me suddenly stop my vehicle that day. Who goes out and gets drunk and passes out while hunting anyway?

That's not a Deer, You Idiot

I know it would have had a huge impact and also be hilarious if I chose to use the actual foul words that this nice old lady was yelling at me in this story. But I decided to keep the stories rather clean so as not to offend anyone. At a certain point of this investigation, I almost gave up. But I don't give up easily. I hardly ever give up. Especially when I know I am right. I have often said that when someone is sure about what they know or believe in, it is very hard to change their mind. This works the same for me. And it is a good thing that I am so strong-minded because if I wasn't, I wouldn't have made this case.

Warm temperatures and an all out pouring rain greeted hunters on this particular opening day of firearms deer season. While patrolling, I received a trespassing complaint about a hunter who was heading in the direction of an old farmhouse on M-19 near Brockway.

Already soaking wet from my earlier contacts, I drove up the drive to the house and walked up to the uncovered porch. I knocked and knocked and knocked. Then, through the downpour of rain, I noticed a skinned out deer hanging in a nearby lean-to shed. The rain was coming down in buckets; one of those diagonal rains. Due to the heavy rain, I could barely make out the silhouette of the hanging deer. Then, a nice, short, old, foreign lady answered the door. Without an invite inside, I stood in the pouring rain and asked her questions about the trespasser, as she stood there warm and dry, inside her house with the door partially open. I asked her about the trespasser again, and her reply in broken English was "Oh, I don't know. You go now." I then asked her who shot the deer. "What deer?" she said. "That deer," I said to which she replied, "That's not a deer, that's a sheep you dumb a**." The nice, old, foreign lady just turned into a rude, old foreign woman. After some insisting, we walked out to the shed and I looked at the skinned animal and stated, "Ma'am that looks like a young deer to me." "That's a lamb you stupid

37

a** hole!" she exclaimed. In broken English she proceeded to almost charge at me while yelling, "You son of a b*****, you mother f***** and what the h*** is wrong with you?! That's a sheep! We raise the sheep. We eat the sheep. See right there!" as she pointed to dozens of live sheep in the attached barn. So yes, it was very believable that the skinned animal could be a sheep, but I still thought that the animal was a deer. I again asked, "Who shot the deer?". "That's not a deer you idiot" she yelled. She would raise her arm up at me and bring her thumb, index finger and middle finger together as if she was crossing herself or saying a prayer. She would shake her hand at me and continued yelling at me over and over. She called me every swear word in the book.

After awhile, I began to question my determination that the animal was a deer. Someone so upset, so convincing, along with the fact that I **was** standing in a sheep barn, lended credence to the old woman's story and was quickly eroding my confidence. But again, I would look at the skinned carcass and conclude that it was a deer.

"You go now, you a** hole, son of a b****! You don't know anything! That's a sheep! We raise the sheep. We eat the sheep, you idiot". Just then, I noticed a single wheelbarrow track leading from the animal in question to an area behind the barn. The track led to a wheelbarrow. Inside the wheelbarrow was a deer head, deer hide, and deer legs. Even though I respect my elders, and I like older people, I did not like this particular one. I looked her in the eyes and yelled, "Quit lying to me and quit swearing at me!". Then I said, "That's not a sheep, it's a deer you stupid a**" (not really, just kidding). I should have called her a idiot and a b****, but I stayed professional and respectful.

The deer happened to be a fawn buck. I then instructed the foul-mouthed senior citizen to contact the poacher and to have him respond to our location. A mild mannered, quiet, and respectful relative of the rude woman showed up. We had a very cordial conversation. The old lady became very meek and docile and offered no more resistance or insults, so I told her "You go now!" The poacher gave me a written confession, and I did arrest him for killing an illegal deer and for trespassing. The errant hunter thanked me for treating him well, and also apologized for the behavior of the rude old lady.

Although I was soaking wet and frustrated, I was proud of the case that I had just made. I returned to my patrol truck and continued working, and I laughed until my cheeks were numb as I thought about how the old woman treated me and about the crude things that she said to me.

Driving While Blacked Out

Many poachers and criminals do their dirty work at night. The cover of darkness helps conceal the movement and activity of bad guys. Since a lot of poaching goes on at night, officers must also work at night. Working late night hours has many rewards for conservation officers. Many serious cases are made during night patrols.

One method of working at night is to drive around the backroads while the headlights are off (also known as being blacked out). Another is to use a small military style sneak light to shine a very small light onto the road in front of your patrol unit. The sneak light is usually not bright enough to scare off a poacher in the distance. I preferred the blacked out method. Now let's forget about the driving without lights policy or the assumed liability for possible accidents caused by driving around at night with headlights shut off.

On a moonlit night, I could drive around for hours at a time with my headlights turned off and my brake lights disabled. On these nights, I could see perfectly using the moonlight as I searched for poachers. On other nights, when the sky was cloudy or during early moon phases, in order to drive dark, along with using my excellent night vision, I would have to feel the crown of the gravel road to help keep me on the road. On many occasions, I would notice a vehicle with poachers shining from their vehicle, and I would drive without lights right up behind the suspects. When I was only 10 to 15 feet behind the violator's vehicle, I would hit my flashers. It would be too late for the poachers to throw their gun out of their window or try to evade me. This was a very effective way to stop deer shiners.

One late night patrol found me northbound on a hardpan gravel road. About three miles away to the northeast, I picked up a glimpse of the light from a spotlight that flashed across the black night sky. It was a very dark night and I was able to get my eyes adjusted to the darkness quite easily. I had my lights off, but my night vision was on. The spotlight again bounced across the sky northeast of my location. I did not want to lose the poachers, so I increased my lights out speed. I drove faster and faster while still mostly just feeling the road. Now, driving maybe 50 to 60 miles per hour, I began closing the distance to the possible poachers. The spotlight beam would dart across the sky similar to the quick flash that is visible when we see a shooting star. My adrenaline was building.

All of a sudden, right in front of me, I saw something. Only a few feet in front of me I made out the shape of a vehicle driving right at me without its headlights on!

I swerved and crashed across an open ditch, then fishtailed and spun to an abrupt stop. Miraculously, I crashed without rolling over or hitting a tree. Shaken but unhurt, I turned my headlights on and drove back up onto the road and chased the Ford truck down. I pulled the truck over and walked up to the driver's window. I was anxious to get a look at the guy that ALMOST just killed me. It was two old drunk guys! They told me they had an electrical problem and that their headlights did not work. So instead of calling for help, they decided to drive home on the back roads as fast as they could so as not to get caught driving drunk. What a stupid plan.

What are the chances that I would be driving blacked out on the same road as some drunk fool driving blacked out and with both of us going too fast? Years of police pursuit driving schools and years of practicing driving without lights at night, along with my good vision and good reflexes saved all of our lives that night. The two drunk stooges ended up in trouble instead of dead. To this day I can't believe I avoided the head-on collision, but still see the need for driving while blacked out, sort of.

Secret Hiding Place

Poachers often hide illegal fish and game. Surprise? Poachers hide deer in vehicles, in buildings, and out in the woods. One of my cases involved the suspects hiding the head and hide from an illegal deer down in a deep hole full of maggots in hopes of getting rid of the illegal evidence. Fishermen hide fish in coolers, clothing, and even hide them in gas tanks. Some poachers cut the bottom out of gas tanks to make a hiding compartment that looks like a gas tank. Other poachers even hide fish down in their waders.

When someone intentionally hides illegal fish, birds, animals, or guns, they quickly get out of the category of possibly getting a warning. There is no room for excuses like, "I did not know the law," "it was an accident," or "I didn't understand the laws." It's like an admission!

Finding hidden fish, game, or guns makes it much easier on the officer. No decision has to be made about if the subjects are going to get arrested. The simple rule is, hidden fish or game equals no warnings.

Such was the case one night when I stopped a 19-foot aluminum boat with three friends on it. It turns out that the men were all college friends who were spending the night fishing as a bachelor's party celebration. The owner of the boat was getting married the next day.

I was checking fishing activity and had checked several boats. Most of the fishermen were targeting walleye. Speaking of walleyes, what a fickle fish they are. Some nights they really bite, some nights they don't bite at all. When the walleyes are biting, they really bite. When the walleye fishing was good, I would work as many hours as possible, and many nights I would stay out all night long trying to do as much as I could to protect our resources. I soon found that most of the fishermen were very happy and had caught their limit of walleye and would soon be heading home with some excellent table fare.

I then checked the one boat that had three college buddies in it. The fishermen told me that they had caught their limit of 18 walleyes. "Great job," I said and then I asked if I could see their fish. They showed me 18 beautiful four to five pound walleye. The subjects were very calm and at ease as we talked about the great weather and the beautiful resources.

Then the look in one of the subject's eyes raised my suspicions. It's hard to describe, but the human eye often acts as a lie detector. The subjects' eyes were telling me something different than what their mouths were telling me. The fishermen kept telling me that they only got 18 walleyes, but their eyes were telling me otherwise. A couple of times, I caught the eyes of the suspects glance toward the back of the boat. I kept making small talk with the subjects, and then I asked them if I could check around in their boat to make sure that there were no extra fish. "Go ahead," and "sure," were the fishermen's answers.

I focused on the rear of the boat. I then searched around the coolers, coats, and tackle and found no hidden fish. Almost ready to give up, I then picked up another sign from the suspects' eyes. I zeroed in on the spot that their eyes directed me to, but there was nothing but riveted down deck material. I ran my hand along the riveted seams of the deck. As I was feeling along the seams, I hit the jackpot. The top that was riveted down from the factory moved when I touched it. It wasn't riveted down. I lifted up on it and found a hidden compartment full of walleye. The subjects had removed the rivets and then glued the heads of the rivets back on to make the panel look like it was still permanently attached.

The fish poachers immediately became very meek and mild tempered. They got beat! Maybe it was out of embarrassment, or maybe it was out of respect for me being able to find the secret hidden fish spot, but nevertheless the fishermen became very calm and friendly. They knew that I was going to hammer them hard. I had no sympathy for the poor soon to be wed poacher and his friends. I ticketed the subjects for the gross over-limit of walleye. I felt very proud of myself for finding the secret hidden compartment. I often wonder how many fish are hidden in other boats.

Old Fashioned Justice

For deer hunters, there is something special about the night before opening day. Preseason planning, target shooting, scouting, and preparing hunting blinds all add to the impending excitement. Many hunters travel long distances. Many hunters meet with family and friends to set up "deer camp." Gear, food, and clothing are organized and ready for opening day. For so many hunters, looking forward to opening day has similar feelings as children looking forward to Christmas. Instead of having visions of sugarplums dancing in their heads, many hunters have visions of huge bucks in their heads. With the planning and preparation done, the night before opening day is usually filled with excitement and anticipation.

One year, I was patrolling for illegal activity and for anyone who tried to cheat and start early. I got a complaint from a family who thought that their 40 acres of woods was quiet and ready for opening morning. Not so much though. The callers told me that someone had entered their woods. The trespasser was pretending he was raccoon hunting when he was just trying to scare deer out of the forest and onto the adjacent property where the trespasser hunted. Wow, if it were true, that would be a rude and harmful act I thought. I called the landowners, and they advised me that the trespasser had parked his white Ford Ranger truck near their woods, and was wandering all around yelling and shouting on their private land. The callers were very upset, almost fighting mad at the trespasser for trying to scare deer from their woods.

So I headed toward the location of the trespassing situation. I was traveling northbound and was about four miles away from the callers' property when I spotted a white Ford Ranger truck coming southbound toward me. Yes, the truck matched the description of the trespasser's truck, but I was not sure that I wanted to stop the white truck and chance missing out on the trespasser's truck. But when the truck passed by me, I changed my mind. When I looked at the driver, I got a gory surprise. His face was all covered in blood. The sight of the bright red blood on the man's face looked like something out of a horror movie.

I decided to stop the truck for two reasons. One, to see if the truck belonged to the trespasser, but secondly and more importantly, to find out why the driver of the truck looked like he was bleeding to death. I spun around and pulled up behind the truck. I then pulled the truck over. As I was walking up toward the driver's window, the driver's door opened and out stumbled a bleeding man in hunting clothes. He had his hand over his nose and was yelling, "Those jerks punched me in the nose, they broke my nose."

The blood was pouring down the man's face as I began to figure out what had happened. I checked him over to see if he needed me to call an ambulance, then I asked him to tell me what had happened, even though I had a pretty good idea myself. The bloody man started going on and on about the jerks who beat him up. I asked, "Oh, where were you at when they beat you up?" He abruptly stated that he was trespassing in the guys' woods and the guys caught him. Then the landowners beat him up for chasing the deer out of their woods. I laughed, I mean, I looked at the trespasser and got all his information and told him to stay in his truck on the side of the road for a few minutes while I went to talk to the landowners who assaulted the trespasser. After interviewing all parties involved, I had to make a decision on who to arrest. Trespassing and assault were both misdemeanor offenses. But my decision was easy. You see, both parties were kind of happy.

a) The trespasser knew that he was wrong.

b) The landowners knew that they were wrong for punching the trespasser.

Both sides were wrong, but considering the fact that it was the night before the firearm deer season opener, and knowing how much preparation the landowners had done and how much anticipation they had built up, I sided with them. I felt that the trespasser deserved what he got. Old fashioned justice prevailed.

Neither party wanted to press charges against the other. The situation was handled properly in the woods, and I did not have to write any tickets, or do any paperwork, or have to go to court, or have to do any computer work. Oh, I wish that I could have lived in the good old days.

Needle in a Haystack

Conservation officers are on the hunter's mind a lot. When people are hunting or poaching, they think about the game warden, especially if they are poaching. They wonder what tree we are hiding behind. They think we are everywhere and any minute, we might jump out. Poachers look at low flying airplanes, thinking that they are DNR spotting officers. Poachers even drive by the local conservation officers' homes to check to see if the patrol truck is at home. It's nice when legal hunters also think of conservation officers often. When they see or hear of possible poaching, they often think of a single officer, in hopes that they can call that officer for help. It is nice to know we are thought of often.

There are other times that we are thought of which are not so obvious. This story involves a lost hunter who was freezing to death and wishing John Borkovich could find him and save him.

One night, St. Clair County dispatch received a 911 cell phone call from a lost and very cold hunter. Dispatch contacted me and also sent several of their units and summoned the Grant and Burtchville Township Fire Departments to respond to the location of the lost hunter. Several of us first responders met at the lost hunter's vehicle. It is amazing how much compassion and regard for human life that our law enforcement and fire department personnel have. We all rushed to the scene to eagerly begin braving the bitter cold in search of the lost man. We set up a command post, and along with police, firemen, and ambulance personnel on standby, we plotted our strategy. One more call from the hunter came into 911 where he stated that his phone battery was dying and that he was also dying, he was getting very cold and was going to lie down.

My brother Mike (also a Michigan Conservation Officer at the time) was patrolling with me as we met all the emergency first responders and expressed our concern about the subject's survival chances if we could not find him soon. For several hours you see, the temperature was six degrees Fahrenheit, and there was a 30 mile an hour northeast wind blowing. The wind chill could soon become deadly.

We all searched and searched the rugged terrain along the Black River. The hunter was lost somewhere out there in some of the thickest, wildest habitat for miles around. The absence of snow only harmed our efforts of trying to locate the man. Now, very dark and getting colder, we felt a sense of urgency as we checked and searched the area. No luck again was the response from the other search teams. We all met back at the command post that we had set up near the waiting ambulance.

I told the firemen and police that my brother Mike and I would take a team of searchers and (thinking out of the box) go in the complete opposite direction from where the subject thought he was. We walked a mile or so and slowly searched the autumn olive and multiflora rose thickets for the poor guy. Every once in awhile we would stop and listen for possible distress calls. We were all tangled up in a massive multi floral rose infestation when we stopped to listen again.

My brother Mike said, "Everyone hold still, I hear a voice ahead of us." Sure enough, we could hear a faint "help me" and "John, John," coming from the tangle ahead of us. Oh my, I felt like someone just gave me million dollars. I swelled up with pride at the fact that the dying man was crying out my name for his salvation. We anxiously walked and crawled into the brush, and from about 15 to 20 feet away, we heard, "John, is that you?" Then we slowly and excitedly made it to the missing hunter.

The freezing man had curled up into the fetal position and was suffering from hypothermia, and later told us that he believed that he was going to die in that spot and knew his life was over. He looked at us and said, "John, I knew if anyone could find me, it would be you." That sure made me feel proud. It's a really good feeling to know that hunters, fishermen, and outdoors people rely on us so much. We touch a lot of lives in so many different ways. We took the freezing man to the waiting ambulance, and all gave each other high fives for another job well done. The appreciative hunter did send a thank you letter to all the firemen, and to my brother and me for saving his life. Getting to him was like finding a needle in a haystack but more rewarding!

John,

Who could have thought on the night, that a misguided neighbor reported to you, I had shot a deer in my back yard. That the next time we would meet, you would be called upon to lead an awesome group of guys to find me lost in the woods of northern st. Clair county.

When my uncle went to a house to call for help, the people there were very kind and helpful, but also very sure he would get very little if not no help at all from the authorities in the area. By the end of the night their opinion had greatly changed.

John I'm a Christian, and you're a professional. And I believe you being there that night was no accident or coincidence. I believe God hand picked you for the job of finding me. I also no why He picked you. I'm not sure of the exact words your Brother spoke that night, but they were something to the effect that if there were a needle that needed to be found out there in those woods, you were the man to find it, and this very over weight needle thanks you and your Brother for your hard work and diligence in coming to my rescue and proving the neighbors wrong.

May God bless two awesome brothers
And their families

Robert Scott Pullman

Robert Scott Pullman
Marysville Mi.

Letter from the lost hunter who was saved from freezing to death by the author and his brother Mike.

Stolen Newspaper Boxes

For years, criminals and litterbugs have thrown objects off bridges and into the rivers and creeks below. Dead bodies, guns, and other evidence often get thrown into the water in an attempt to get rid of it. Tossing things off bridges has become such a common occurrence that one never knows what might be found in the water below the bridges.

One day under one of the bridges, I found something out of the ordinary. I found a metal newspaper vending machine box in the Black River. The box was almost four feet tall and was very heavy, so I thought the box might have been part of a prank. Then a few days later I found another box belonging to the *Port Huron Times Herald*, then another one from to the *Detroit News*. I pulled one of the boxes out of the river and discovered that the coin box had been sawed out and that the money was missing. Now, don't laugh, I thought the same thing, stealing a paper box, cutting open the coin box and taking the box out in the country to throw it in the river, just for a few quarters? I checked with the newspaper and found out that sometimes the boxes would hold $30 to $40 worth of quarters. Still, not much money for all of the work, not to mention the lack of care and the disregard for our rivers.

I kept finding more boxes in rivers and creeks, and each time I would think to myself, for all of the hard work and hours involved in stealing, cutting open, then transporting the boxes, and then throwing them into the river, these guys could make way more money flipping burgers.

Oh, but flipping burgers is an honest job performed by honest people. Two separate store owners called to report their paper boxes had been stolen and one of the store owners told the St. Clair County Sheriff Department that at 4:00 a.m., she saw a dark van speeding away after loading a newspaper box. Months went by and more boxes were thrown into our creeks and rivers. *The Port Huron Times Herald* and the *Detroit Free Press* advised me that each box costs approximately $600 to purchase. The number of paper boxes thrown into the river grew to 49 boxes. Now the thefts were totaling thousands of dollars. But what I was even more mad about was the disregard these criminals had for our environment. The blatant lack of care for our waters, fish, and wildlife was getting me upset.

As I tried to understand what kind of case I was working on and how to solve it, several questions remained unanswered. Why would someone spend so much time stealing the paper boxes, driving them home, cutting open the change box, then driving out to the river? The number of hours of labor, the fuel costs and the wear and tear on the suspects' vehicle must have exceeded the amount of money the suspects were stealing from the newspaper boxes.

So I wondered, were they taking the boxes for the money or were these people just plain criminals?

As an officer, it is fun to set out on a mission. It's fun to plan and prepare to catch one particular criminal, similar to the TV show, "First 48", where they try to solve a murder case.

An officer must think deeply and use advanced tactics to catch some criminals, and that's where the fun is. It is almost a game, me against them! A chess game of sorts. I have to work harder, be quicker thinking, and use "police intuition" to be able to out think or out maneuver a criminal.

Some cases take a lot of time and energy to solve. This particular one took months of patrolling and old fashioned spot and stalk police work to make.

Upon finding the dumping grounds of the stolen newspaper boxes, I knew that the bad guys would be back to dump more. The problem was that they were dumping them in rivers and creeks in about ten different spots spread out over a 10 square mile area. I could not be at 10 different places at the same time, all day and all night. So for weeks, along with my regular deer, fish, ORV, and miscellaneous patrols, meetings, and training, I would drive (aggressively) around the dumping ground area as often as I could. I would keep checking the rivers and creeks- trying to catch the thieves, and at the same time protecting our resources.

I vowed (to my police friends and to myself), to catch these criminals and to save our rivers. I spent many hours guarding the bridges and rivers. Then, one dark night in September, I approached the M-136 bridge over the Black River. I saw a vehicle stopped on the bridge. I was still one-third of a mile away, so I floored my patrol truck and zoomed up to the bridge.

Going a little too fast, I had to slam on the brakes to stop in time. As I was skidding to a stop, I saw a male suspect throwing a large, blue metal newspaper box into the river. At the same time, the driver of the dark van was frantically and hysterically yelling to the other suspect,

The author and St. Clair County Deputy Jeff Green surveying some of the 54 newspaper boxes dumped into our rivers.

"Hurry up, hurry up, hurry up, a car is coming." Too late for that, you're mine already, I thought.

I jumped out of my truck and yelled: "Police, don't move." The suspect who had thrown the box was standing on the bridge. He had a pair of work gloves on and murmured something about trying to clean up all of the boxes in the river. He said that he was just a good guy and that he was helping. Busted and caught red-handed, he still tried to lie to me. The dark van still had one blue newspaper box in it.

St. Clair County Sheriff Department Deputy Jeff Green and Michigan Conservation Officer Ben Lasher did respond to my location. We gathered evidence and had Preferred Towing load the suspects' van and tow it away. We even searched the suspects' home and shed and found more boxes and a cutting tool with several coin boxes that had been cut out. I arrested the suspects on several felony charges. In all, I retrieved 54 newspaper boxes with total losses of over $32,000 thousand dollars just in stolen property. This total doesn't even include the amount of money that was taken from inside of the boxes. I also arrested the suspects for some serious littering violations.

With the help of the SCCSD Deputy Jeff Green, the Drain Commissioner Bob Wiley, and one of his employees, (former Marine, Ron Kincaid), we waded into the river and pulled all of the boxes out and returned them to their owners. I also returned our rivers to the deserving owners, the citizens of the state of Michigan. Some criminals put a lot of thought and planning into their crimes, and many times they can avoid being arrested. The biggest mistake these criminals made was throwing the metal boxes into our rivers. That decision offended me and set me on a course to stop them.

The next time you are traveling over a river, stream, or creek, glance down and take a moment to wonder what has been thrown into the river over the years.

I Shot the Doe

An officer never knows what is waiting at the next corner, vehicle stop, or public contact. Maybe many of us officers have Attention Deficit Disorder because we need to be multitasking all the time and constantly thinking in many different directions. All the while, looking for clues, arresting suspects, listening and dealing with multiple suspects and coping with varying situations. Upon any stop an officer's mind may be computing the following: white truck, man with a gun, blood on the tailgate, passenger moving all around, handgun ammo on console, smell of marijuana, beer can spilling, passing vehicle right behind me, gunshot to the north, and many other sights, sounds, and smells. Sorting out each stop or contact is a monumental task. Trying to figure out what the suspects are doing or doing wrong is very critical in police work. Sometimes what an officer thinks a suspect is doing wrong turns out to be something entirely different. This story contains details about one of these interesting and confusing interactions.

October 20th was always the opening day of pheasant season. Opening day was almost sacred. The excitement and anticipation on the first day of season was unbelievable.

Pheasant season opened at 10:00 a.m. opening day during this era. Pheasant hunters young and old would eagerly and excitely wait for the season to open. The wait was similar to how people countdown the time at a New Year's Eve celebration.

One year when I was patrolling on opening day, I saw two hunters standing near the back of their pickup truck. Then they closed the topper on their truck when they saw me approaching. I pulled up and asked them if they had had any luck. They said no. I glanced at the back of the truck, and I noticed a small drop of blood on the tailgate latch. I again asked, "Did you get any pheasants?" The answer was no again. I asked if I could take a

52

look in the back of their truck and the older of the two men came completely unglued. He started confessing out loud and with tears running down his face, said, "I shot the Doe." Over and over he kept saying, "I shot the doe. I shot the doe." I replied, "It's alright sir, it's going to be alright." "I shot the doe," was all that he could say. I then asked if I could see inside their truck topper to see the illegal deer. The subject opened up the back of the truck topper. I looked under the hunting coats and boots but I could not see the doe. I asked where the doe was and the old Italian fella said, "In the bucket." Now, I'm thinking that it must be a small deer to fit inside of a five-gallon bucket, or maybe just the meat was in the bucket.

I pulled the bucket out and inside of it, was a hen pheasant! My deer case now morphed into a pheasant case. The hunter kept apologizing and showed great remorse for killing the hen (doe) pheasant.

I sort of believed the old guy when he explained to me that he had shot the "doe" by accident. To his credit, at least he did not just throw the illegal pheasant into the weeds to let it rot. Due to his old age and how upset he was, the amount of remorse that he had, and how respectful he was to me, I only wrote the hunter a ticket for the most minimal violation possible.

The John Deere Deer

All of us have heard a single gunshot during archery season. As we sit there not seeing any deer, it's easy to connect the dots and assume that the deer we did not see, just got shot by a poacher. In reality, many of these shots are just someone shooting at a squirrel, raccoon, or just target shooting. Maybe 90-95% of these shots are harmless, but often in my woods and yours we know someone just poached a deer.

This story is about a group of hunters who heard a rifle shot and knew the neighbor had just shot the big eight-point buck that they saw run from their land and into their neighbor's woods. On November 10th, just five days before the firearms deer season opener, I received a complaint of a possible poaching incident that happened in the Emmett area. The caller and his two hunting buddies told me that they had been bow hunting on their farm. Just before dark, they saw a big eight-point buck travel across their cut soybean field. As soon as the buck entered their neighbor's woods, they heard a single shot. After awhile, the complainants saw a flashlight and saw someone who looked like he was dragging something in the woods. The callers told me that they had had problems with their neighbors trespassing in the past. The suspect neighbors were foreign, and according to the callers, the suspects might be Hamon members of the Asian community. Coupled with the fact that I would possibly be confronting blatant armed trespassers and based on the very sad situation that happened in Wisconsin four years earlier where a Hamon hunter was trespassing and killed seven members of one Wisconsin family, the situation was anything but stable.

I radioed for backup. I very seldom requested police backup when I arrested poachers, but whenever I did, the other police officers knew there was not any crying wolf involved and would try to give me quick and good backup help. One St. Clair County deputy responded with me on foot while two other cars responded and waited about three-quarters of a mile away near the suspect's home. I had the callers walk us back to the area of the possible poaching. Now, being well after dark, we found blood and then some drag marks on the November leaves. We followed the drag marks towards the suspect's home and eventually ended up at the back door of his home. I could see several rifles and shotguns laying around inside of the house, and one rifle was leaning up against the back door. Was there going to be an armed encounter? After awhile of knocking, the suspect finally answered the door, and stated when asked about the deer, "No deer, just squirrel hunting." I then looked around and noticed a John Deere lawn mower which had a sled hooked up to it with a rope. I shined my flashlight onto the sled, and I immediately recognized a white deer hair and a little blood. I said, "Oh what's that? That looks like deer hair." The suspect said, "We bow and arrow hunt deer." "Okay" I said, "let's see your bow killed deer," and again was met with the answer, "no deer." I said alright, and I followed the lawnmower tracks, deer blood, and deer hair through the suspect's backyard back toward his woods. I again stated I would like to see the deer. He said, "No deer" again. Finally, the suspect walked with me about 300 yards behind his house to where the squirrel (oops, eight-point buck) laid. The only problem was that the big buck had a small caliber rifle bullet hole in it.

The suspect told me how he shot the eight-point with a rifle and showed me a second eight-point buck that he also shot with a rifle. He then gave me a confession about how he killed the deer during bow season with a .17 caliber rifle and how he hid the bigger buck behind his house.

Eventually, the suspect was very cooperative and respectful and in no way showed any indication that was like the murderer trespasser in the sad Wisconsin incident. The poacher did have a large garden. He even sold vegetables commercially. Even though he was polite and friendly and all, the poacher went a little too far when he tried to convince me that he was killing deer just to keep them out of his garden. It was a poor and feeble attempt coming from a guy who shot two big eight-point bucks with a rifle in bow season! After gathering evidence and obtaining a written confession, I walked back to my patrol truck. In the woods, I could see three subjects sitting on their ORV's watching every move that I was making! It was the complainants. They did not even care or try to hide from the poacher. They were not even concerned about possible retaliation or had any fear from the old fashioned "barn burning" scare tactic. All they cared about was that the poacher would get caught and that I would be safe.

These three guys exemplified many of our great hunters. They just wanted to hunt legally and did not want to be bothered by trespassers and poachers. They had so much conviction on how they felt that they did not even care that the whole world knew who reported the poaching. I shook their hands over and over for not just calling me and for being law-abiding hunters, but also for their "fearless, do the right thing approach" to hunting and to life. Good does prevail, evil does lose, and great hunters like my three new friends prove to me once again that there are so many good people hunting and fishing here in Michigan.

White Bronco

Most of us remember the white Ford Bronco that O.J. Simpson was driving as the police chased him all over California a few years back. Well, I had my own very serious encounter with a big white Ford Bronco.

It was a dark, cold October night one year when I found a full-size white Ford Bronco parked in a lane near a large woodlot. It had been dark for hours already, and along with the fact that I had received poaching complaints in this exact area, I decided to invest some time checking the area.

I hid my patrol truck about one-quarter a mile away and parked blacked out in total darkness. After a while, I spotted a flashlight out in the field near the woods. It was such a dark night and I was so far away that even with my 10x50 binoculars, I couldn't tell exactly what the subject with the flashlight was doing. In my mind, I knew he had an illegal deer.

I patiently watched as the flashlight began getting closer to the parked Bronco. Now being only the distance of a football field, I still could not decipher what was going on. Unfortunately, cold October nights would always fog my windshield. Defroster on, defroster off. Heat then cold, oh, nothing was working, and it was getting frustrating trying to see the illegal deer the poacher was dragging.

Through my binoculars, all I could see was the silhouette of a person walking very slowly with a flashlight. When the subject made it all the way to the Bronco, the dome light came on, and then the poacher opened the rear door. In one motion, he threw something into the vehicle. I saw a flash of white but could not see much else (the white must have been the white belly hair of the illegal deer).

Soon, the Bronco backed out onto the gravel road and took off rather quickly to the south. I emerged from my hiding spot and rushed up behind the suspect's vehicle. I hit my blue lights and cast my spotlight into the vehicle's interior. Unfortunately (or fortunately) the driver in the O.J. Simpson looking vehicle did not flee. The white Bronco came to a stop. Confident of a good poaching case, I proudly walked up toward the driver's door.

An "officer's bliss" came over me as I asked the visibly shaking suspect, "How are you doing tonight?" The nervous driver stated, "You got me." The subject's voice was cracking and he was so upset as he said, "I'm sorry," then hung his head in shame. I calmly said, "It's OK, it will be alright," then I asked to see inside the back of the Bronco.

At this point, I still had not seen any blood, hair, or the deer's body, but was still confident in my assessment of the situation. I asked for the subject's driver's license, then walked with him to the back of the SUV.

The defeated subject walked the walk of shame, then slowly opened the rear latch and dropped the tailgate. The poor guy again apologized for his wrongdoing. I anxiously looked into the vehicle and my jaw dropped. There was no deer. But right there, right in front of me, was a white five-gallon plastic bucket full of dirty potatoes. Oh my, the suspect was not out poaching deer, he was out stealing potatoes. You see, the 40-acre field adjacent to the woodlot was a potato field.

I was dumbfounded. I had to make a decision. Should I arrest the father of three for stealing $8.00 worth of muddy potatoes or not? Well, let's just say the compassionate side of me came out once again. I told him not to steal any more potatoes and to be careful driving home.

Ultimate Life and Death Judgement

Michigan Conservation Officers have many duties and responsibilities. One of these duties pertains to the use of deadly force. As with all other peace officers, a heavy load is placed on us regarding when to use a firearm to take someone's life. Lethal force may be used to save an officer's life or that of another person. There are plenty of laws, policies, and directives used to determine when it is appropriate to end someone's life. However, when is it permissible to end the life of an injured animal?

One task assigned to Conservation Officers is to respond to humanely dispatch injured or sick animals. For instance, many deer (50,000 per year) in Michigan are hit by vehicles. Many of the deer are badly injured but still alive after the accident. Peace officers around the state have almost all been called on to stop the suffering of a deer after it was hit by a car.

I remember the first time my wife Nancy ever patrolled with me back in 1989. As we were driving along, I could see three vehicles on the shoulder of the road ahead with their four-way hazard lights on. As we approached the scene, I noticed that one of the vehicles had a damaged grill, and broken headlight. I could see a small deer trying to move as it tried to get off of the road. I told my wife that I would examine the deer and if it was injured as bad as it looks, I would have to shoot the poor deer to put it out of its misery and to end its suffering. As I walked up to the young deer, I could see it had a broken back and was crying out loud, it was unable to move its hind legs, and the deer's intestines had ripped open from the collision. I quickly decided to shoot the deer and turned around to see the driver and my wife crying. I sadly shot the deer then reholstered my gun. When we drove away, all my wife said was that she felt so bad for the deer but understood that I had to do what I did. I told her that it breaks my heart to have to kill an injured deer, even though it is my obligation to respond and to end the animal's suffering.

What a heavy responsibility to carry around, knowing with my decision only that I make the judgment call on which animals to put down. Quite similar to when a veterinarian advises a family to euthanize a pet, a sad but necessary decision needs to be made. Oh, how I wish I could somehow heal these poor suffering animals, but I am called on to do the next best thing.

Hooked to Beer Cans, Sticks, and Bottles

Catching poachers is similar to putting together a difficult puzzle. An officer needs to fit the right pieces of evidence and clues together in order to solve the crime. Sometimes, it becomes very difficult to get the last piece of the puzzle to fit. Often an officer knows the suspects are guilty and needs just one more piece of information to make the case. One such case involved a group of fishermen who always caught way more fish than all of the other fishermen.

The Trumpeter Swans were flying north, a sure sign that winter had ended. For the first time all year, I saw Turkey Vultures circling overhead as they looked for dead animals. An early spring rain had brought suckers in from Lake Huron into the tributaries that fed the lake. The suckers being caught were very large Red Horse and Great Lakes suckers. Most of the people that were sucker fishing were catching four or five apiece. One group of fishermen, however, had hundreds of suckers. Proportionately, they had markedly more fish than anyone else that I had checked. Probably just good at fishing, I thought. The subjects packed up their gear and hauled out the multitude of fish that they had caught. I pondered the good luck that the fishermen had had.

The next time I encountered the same group, they had grossly out-fished the other fishermen in the area again. I decided to spend a little time to watch the subjects the next time that they were fishing. At the time, the maximum number of fishing rods a person could use at one time was two per person. I mention this because the next time I saw the group fishing, all five of the subjects had two fishing rods propped up on forked sticks in front of them. Totally legal to the naked eye.

I observed the subjects messing around with some fishing line and some sticks and one of subjects grabbed a stick and pulled a fish in. I watched another subject tying line to some beer cans on the ground near him. All the while that they were messing around with the beer cans and the fishing line, I could see their two legal fishing rods right in front of them. Then I saw one of the subjects pulling on some line, and he pulled in a fish that wasn't even near the two rods he had propped up in front of him. When I approached the subject, I commented about how many fish they were catching. The fisherman stated, "Yeah, they're really biting on our two lines that we are using." Just then, a beer can from in the woods began moving toward the river. I grabbed the beer can and found a fishing line hooked to it. There was a fish on the other end of the line. As I was pulling in the fish, I looked around at the subjects' surprised faces. Then I noticed a potato chip bag moving toward the river. I grabbed the potato chip bag and pulled in another fish.

These cunning fishermen put a lot of thought and work into their illegal scheme, and from a distance, their plan worked. But I soon found dozens and dozens and dozens of pieces of litter such as bottles, cans, plastic, sticks, and stones being used as set lines. I gave them an A for effort and a ticket for fishing with too many lines.

Saturday Night Special

As a law enforcement officer looks back on his or her career, several close calls with death are always at the back of our mind. I have had several close calls ranging from car accidents, police chases, traffic stops, traffic control, water and ice rescues, lightning strikes, and encountering suspects with weapons. Weapons used against police can be of any type, ranging from vehicles, knives, guns, or clubs, to shovels and hammers.

Some of the close calls are closer to death than others. One of my most dangerous incidents where I almost lost my life happened one night while I was patrolling for deer poachers.

While hunting for illegal deer activity one Saturday night at about 10:00 p.m., I heard a radio broadcast of a home invasion that had just occurred. Since the scene was only about four miles away from my location, I quickly responded and met Deputy Steve Rickert at the stated address.

As we began investigating the home invasion, we had three "witnesses" telling us that three guys broke into their parent's home and their neighbor's home. We searched the badly ransacked homes. We found broken windows, broken televisions, and there was glass and debris all over the floors. The phone lines and power lines had all been cut to the homes. We were on location of some serious home invasions.

As we interviewed the witnesses, they kept telling us that the suspects were right here, and that they had red jackets on, and they were big guys, they, they, they. At one point, I got suspicious of the witnesses' stories and focused on one of the subjects. Very politely, I began asking a lot of questions about the home invasions. Then the subject I was talking to made the mistake of saying that he saw the suspect breaking into the houses. He then stated that the suspect ran from the house. I asked him what the suspect was wearing and he said that the suspect had a red jacket on.

I calmly advised the subject that he misspoke several times, and I mentioned the inconsistency of his plural versus singular descriptions. I told him that I was becoming suspicious of him because in the beginning he kept mentioning several bad guys broke in and they they they, and then he switched to saying he did this, he did that, and he looked like that.

After about 25 minutes of accusatory questions directed at the subject, the subject dropped his head and said, "Yeah, we did the break-ins, and we made up the story about the three guys to fool you cops." At that point, I Mirandized the now suspect and asked him about the home invasion and about what he stole. The suspect said that they had taken a lot of money, coins, jewelry, and other items. He admitted that they had cut the phone and power lines. He stated that they had hidden a lot of the stolen items in a boat in the backyard, but that the jewelry and money were taken to a relative's home two doors to the east.

I told the suspect to get into my patrol truck and I would drive him to his relative's to get the stolen items. The suspect calmly said that he would rather walk with me to the house so that we would not scare his grandfather at the house. After doing so well, getting a confession and solving the case, I was on a roll. I was hoping to continue gathering information, so I decided to stay on the "light side" and agreed to walk with the suspect.

While walking the quarter mile in the dark, secluded yard, the suspect stopped and reached into his right front pocket. I immediately said, "Oh, keep your hands out of your pockets." I reached down to the suspect's pocket for a "Terry Pat Down" search for weapons. As I ran my hand over his pocket, I immediately recognized the shape of a handgun. The suspect was now pulling upward in an attempt to pull the gun out in an effort to shoot me! I could not let this happen. I was so close to the suspect that I decided to engage him and fight for the gun instead of pushing him away and just shooting him. Instantly, I reasoned that if I pushed him away then drew my gun, that he already had his gun in his hand and that he might shoot me first. That was not going to happen!

I reached into the suspect's pocket. He had the gun in his hand, and I also grabbed the gun. I tried to pull the trigger and shoot the assailant in the groin and hip area. But the Saturday Night Special was a small .380 auto semi-automatic, and there was not enough room for both of our fingers on the trigger. The fight was on! I then pulled the suspect's hand with the gun still in it from his pocket and then hit him as hard as I could a couple of hundred times (now really, just a couple of times). MY KIND OF GUN CONTROL!

As I roughly placed the felon on the ground, I then threw his loaded illegal handgun to the side. I kept yelling for him to cooperate as I put the idiot in handcuffs. Deputy Rickert heard me yelling and ran over to assist me with the suspect. Oh, how tempting it was to sign up for the police brutality training course and apply some of it to the suspect. Deputy Rickert yelled to the suspect, "Yeah, you want to shoot a cop. How did that work for you?

You lost!!" Detective Dave Patterson also responded to help me. He also told the suspect that he was lucky that I did not shoot him.

What is so shocking (or maybe not) and unbelievable is that after the fool had got out of prison on my charges, he continued his life of crime. Robbery, home invasion, assault, and resisting and obstructing police have all been added to his resume. Maybe I should have pushed him away and used my gun after all.

Currently, he is living comfortably in a jail cell with all meals, clothing, heat, lights, air conditioning, computer access, and all medical and dental care provided with all of the comforts of a bread and breakfast resort all paid for by the rest of us law abiding citizens. Puzzling isn't it?

Photo of subject who attempted to shoot the author with the illegal handgun in the foreground.

"John, It's Me" As I Tackled Him

Ever find a $20.00 bill laying on the ground in a parking lot? Ever find a shed antler? Ever find a giant morel mushroom? How about win $1000.00 on an instant lotto ticket or win the publisher's clearinghouse sweepstakes? There is a heart rush feeling that comes over you, isn't there? It's a surprised and happy feeling that is hard to duplicate.

Well, there are a lot of times during a conservation officer's career when an officer gets this same type of heart rush. Officers spend countless hours searching, seeking, and hunting for real cases. Some days and nights are very, very slow with no activity and then all of a sudden, bingo, Yahtzee, or checkmate. The heart rush is there again!

Sitting on the hood of my patrol truck, I could feel the warmth from the motor, but I could also feel the chill of the October night. From my vantage point, I could look for poachers using spotlights, and at the same time, I could listen for vehicles and gunshots.

Then I got all three. I saw a vehicle shining about one mile away and then I heard a shot. I rushed to the location but the vehicle was out of sight. However, I did see a small flashlight out in the woods. So I busted out of my truck and began running toward the flashlight's location. The subject must have heard me coming because he was not using his flashlight anymore. In the distance, I could hear someone running in the woods. I ran toward the sounds of rustling leaves and twigs snapping, then I stopped and listened. I could still hear the crunching of the suspect's footsteps, so I ran for another couple hundred yards. As I was running, I could smell a dead deer and soon I found a doe lying right in front of me. I stopped long enough to see that the deer had a bullet hole in its neck, and it was a very very freshly killed animal.

Now I knew exactly what had transpired and it gave me even more determination to catch the fleeing poacher. I ran, then stopped, and I ran then stopped several more times. Each time that I stopped, I could tell that I was getting closer.

The poacher was trying to get away without using his flashlight which made it much harder to run quietly. I was yelling for him to stop, all the while closing the gap to a point now where I could see the suspect. As I got closer, I could see the suspect running with a scoped rifle, and soon I was only 20 feet behind him when I yelled again, "Stop, police! You're under arrest! Stop, conservation officer."

Still running and preparing for a crash landing, I heard, "John it's me." I kept running, and as I brought the subject down, I heard him say again, "Oh you know me," and "John it's me." Oh, okay, then it's all okay that you killed a doe at night with a rifle using spotlight and and you're running away from me. I don't think so. After I had tackled him, I stated that I don't care who you are, you are under arrest. Michigan State Police Troopers Matt Laymon and Chris Tuckey soon responded to my location and helped me with the suspect and with evidence, and also with catching the driver of the vehicle involved in the shooting.

Stolen Snowmobile Chase

Chasing machines that travel 140 mph is a daunting thought. I hear from many officers that we can never catch motorcycles, dirt bikes, and snowmobiles. Maybe so, for some officers. But I sort of like the challenge of catching people who have all the odds in their favor. I recall tackling snowmobilers and ORV riders traveling 50 to 60 mph. What was I thinking? Tackling a fleeing suspect or one trying to go around me off of their machine that is going 55 mph may not be the smartest thing I ever did, but I did it lots of times. What kind of madman would tackle a fleeing felon on a snowmobile at 55 miles per hour? Oh, just me.

After almost every chase, I would tell the (once fleeing, now handcuffed) subject that I was not even going to write him a ticket. I was only going to remind him of the violation and educate him about the laws.

Six inches of fresh snow blanketed the ground on this particular Sunday morning. It was January and quite cold out at about 10:00 a.m. when I noticed two snowmobiles coming toward me at a high rate of speed. Riding snowmobiles on county roads was prohibited, so I decided to stop the machines to advise the operators of the law and to check their registrations. I planned to just educate the drivers and have a positive public contact, and let them go with just warnings.

I activated my emergency lights to signal for the approaching snowmobiles to stop. The machines accelerated toward me to try to get around me. I jumped out of my patrol truck and grabbed the coat of the driver on the second snowmobile to try to roll him off of the sled. Somehow, the snowmobile driver going over 55 mph pulled free of my grip (temporarily). The chase was on now. I spun my truck around and grabbed my radio and advised St. Clair County Dispatch that I was in pursuit of two snowmobiles. St. Clair County Deputy Bob Gross immediately called me back on the radio and asked me if one snowmobile was orange and the other one bright green. I answered back while speeding, swerving, slipping, and sliding with my lights and siren on, "That's affirmative."

Deputy Gross advised me that he just sat down with the owners of the two snowmobiles. The owners called to report that someone had stolen their snowmobiles from their home only a few miles away. Deputy Gross was in the process of taking the owners' complaint at the exact time that I called out the chase.

I chased the orange machine. Then it went across a very large open field. I raced to intercept him where I figured he would exit the field. As the suspect drove the stolen snowmobile through a deep ditch and back onto the road, he ran into some bad luck. Me. I then had a positive public contact with the felon. The 20-year-old suspect now laying on the road, began crying.

A few minutes later, his cell phone started ringing. Assuming that the call was from the guy on the second snowmobile, I helped get the man's cell phone out of his pocket since he was already in my silver bracelets. I told my suspect not to tell his friend that I had caught him. Just as I thought, the caller was the suspect's friend who stole the green snowmobile. The second suspect told my handcuffed buddy (as I held his phone to his ear) that the belt had broken on his snowmobile and that he was hiding behind a barn on Foley Road near M-19. Now, along with Deputy Gross and Retired Deputy Ray Gleason (who owned the barn), we followed a snowmobile track behind the barn to the hiding thief standing next to the green snowmobile.

I arrested the suspect for fleeing and eluding police and for the larceny of the snowmobiles. Deputy Gross then excitedly exclaimed, "The snowmobiles were not even reported to LEIN as stolen yet, and John was already chasing them!" How does that saying go? The police are never around when you need them. I guess I was this time, though!

Raccoon Jumped into my Patrol Car

On this warm July afternoon, I decided to patrol around the state land along the Black River in St. Clair County. I checked several Black River and Mill Creek access sites for fishing activity and possible litter violations. Some ignorant people use our state and federal land for dump sites. They discard all types of items ranging from tires to refrigerators to garbage bags. I would check each area several times a day to catch these litterbugs.

As I pulled into a parking area near Mill Creek, I noticed a plastic bag of litter. I exited my vehicle to check the bag's contents. When I was getting back into my car, I started to close my car door, when all of a sudden, a large raccoon ran and jumped into my car. Now what should I do, I thought. Most raccoons are nocturnal. Was this raccoon sick? Did he have rabies or some other animal problem causing him to be out during the middle of the day? Or was the masked bandit a wanted criminal who was just turning himself into me to go to jail? Ha. I tried everything to get him out of my car. Nothing was working- he was not getting out!! There I was, sitting in the front seat with a big, possibly rabid raccoon sitting in the backseat. Was he going to bite me or just take a dump in my car? I did not like either option.

I decided that I would bribe him out with some food, so I quickly drove towards the Ruby store which was only a few miles away. As we were traveling, the masked bandit crawled up the back of my seat and clawed at my head. I couldn't shoot him in my car, but I would have to if he started attacking me although he was too cute to shoot. Then, he curiously reached out and gently touched my ear. Then he sat down next to me. When I got to the store, I flung open the door, ran inside, and bought some beef jerky and cheese packs and some marshmallows.

He loved the food but would not exit my patrol car. He was a cute, chubby little guy. He kept looking right at me and now seemed to have a friendly air about him. Soon, I sat back in my car and my new partner sat on my lap, eating jerky, cheese, and marshmallows. I realized that he must have been someone's pet and that he was very nice. So I took him home to show my wife. He was on my shoulder as I walked into my home on Lake Huron. She laughed, and we petted the raccoon, and we were amused while he walked around our house curiously looking for things. He opened up the kitchen cabinets and checked out everything. Then we showed some of our neighbors our cute new friend. We all played with him and gave him plenty of snacks and attention. I then took my raccoon buddy for a ride about one mile away to Lakeport State Park and let him go. The end, or so I thought.

Two nights later, the telephone rang and jolted me out of a deep sleep at 2:30 a.m. When I said hello, I heard a screaming elderly woman's voice yelling, "John, John, your raccoon is in my bed!". "Settle down ma'am," I said, "What is the problem?" She yelled again, "Your raccoon is in my bed. He came in through my cat door and knocked the lamp off of the night stand, then jumped onto my bed." I quickly responded to help my neighbor. "Come on buddy," I said as I gave him more marshmallows and led him back to his seat in my car. After a longer ride, I released him back into his natural environment.

Deer in Bathtub

Hunters often donate game to families in need. Many hunters belong to groups such as Hunters Feeding the Hungry. Belonging to these groups is a good way to help the less fortunate among us. Conservation officers also help the needy by donating confiscated fish and meat. Many times, I have found needy families on my own. I would search out people who seem to be down on their luck or out of work, or just have a large family and need a little extra help putting food on the table. It is a very rewarding feeling to give people free, fresh, good, organic food. I mention the word fresh for a reason. The deer meat from the following case was not the type I wanted to give out as a goodwill gesture to people in need.

One year while I was out hunting for poachers, I found a spot where someone had dragged a deer out of a woodlot. Since deer season was not open, I began my investigation with excitement. Once I get on the trail of an illegal deer poacher, I work hard to catch up to the culprit.

On this particular deer case, I spent almost all day searching for clues and gathering evidence and interviewing people. Then late in the day, I finally was able to figure out who the suspect was and where he had taken his illegal deer. He had the deer at his house. I quickly responded to the suspect's residence, but the suspect's vehicle was not in the driveway.

I knocked on the door of the saltbox style house, and a young woman answered the door. The woman was very polite and was neat and clean in her appearance. I asked if the suspect was home and the woman said no, but that she was his wife.

I advised her that her husband had shot a deer and that I needed to take a look at the deer. When I asked the cooperative woman where the deer was at, she told me that it was upstairs in the bathtub. At first, I thought that she was just messing with me or possibly trying to get me alone in the upstairs bathroom. More importantly, I began to wonder if I was being set up or something.

Being a little apprehensive and cautious, I followed the woman up the stairs to the second floor; then we walked down the hallway to the bathroom. I slowly opened the bathroom door, and we walked toward the tub. Right there in the bathtub was the illegal deer. However, that was not the most surprising thing. The deer had been mostly skinned, and the entire carcass was soaking in the tub full of water. The tub was full of a bloody slurry of foam, deer hair (and bacteria).

I politely asked the woman why the deer was taking a bubble bath. She advised me that her husband always soaks his deer for three days in lukewarm water to get the blood out.

Oh my, no wonder some people do not like the taste of venison. That was one deer that I did not confiscate to give to a needy family.

Wind Catches Sailors Off Guard

There I was patrolling around in a nice boat. Gas and all boat expenses were paid for me as I was enjoying the water, beaches and fresh air- all the while getting paid!

People would always ask me if I was getting paid to ride around in a boat and I would say "Ya, but someone has to do it, I will suffer through the day".

Yes, most boat patrolling days are spent just riding around enjoying the water and all of the sights.

But, on any given day, the fun, relaxing, and enjoyable boat ride can turn into a harrowing lifesaving situation.

One hot June day I was patrolling lower Lake Huron with my 18.5' aluminum Lund boat. When I was near Lakeport, a strong northeast wind kicked up and brought eight to ten-foot waves within minutes. I headed south toward the safety of Port Huron. The waves were so large that they would crash inside of my boat and knock me around. I could see the swells ahead of me; which would gobble up my boat then push me back up to the crest of the next wave. My bilge pump was not keeping up with the incoming water by now. As I watched the waves ahead of me, one white wave looked different. As I neared the white wave, I realized that it was not even a wave at all, it was a capsized boat. The three occupants had been thrown into the water. One of the boaters was an 81-year-old man, and all three were trying to stay afloat while having only one lifejacket. I began plucking the boaters to safety while still fighting the waves myself. With no boats in sight and no other police boats nearby, I frantically worked to save the three boaters and finally succeeded. I called SCCSD who sent a patrol boat to tow the capsized boat into calmer water. The three rescued boaters were grateful, and we all miraculously made it into safety.

Then, only two months later in August, I heard a BOL broadcast about two armed robbers who used a .357 magnum handgun to rob a store and then escaped in a black Monte Carlo. Only seconds later, I saw the suspects' car with the matching license plate on it.

The Monte Carlo was westbound on Lapeer Road west of Wadhams. I did a U-turn and tried to stop the vehicle at which time the vehicle fled then turned into a drive and the two occupants jumped out and started running. The passenger did stop and was placed into handcuffs near the vehicle. I got into a foot chase with the other suspect and soon had backup from the St. Clair County Sheriff Department and the Michigan State Police. I spotted the suspect hiding behind an outbuilding in the woods and then tackled the suspect to the ground. After the suspect was in custody, we transported him back to the party store so that the store clerk could make positive identification. The ironic part is that the owners of the party store happened to be the three capsized boaters that I rescued in June. The store owner called me their guardian angel.

Then, being hot and tired from the foot chase, I got a cold Pepsi from the cooler and placed it on the counter. The clerk said, "$1.00 please." I gladly paid the for the pop but had to chuckle to myself on the way out of the store. I thought to myself that I don't do this job for free pop, money, or glory, I just do it because it is the right thing to do!

Illegal Immigrants Poaching our Deer

Why would a single officer attempt to arrest six trespassing poachers dressed in full camouflage and carrying rifles all by himself? I don't know why. But I did it. It was dangerous and stupid, but fun though.

Riding around during deer season in my patrol truck was something extra special. I would drive and drive, hunting for game law violators. It was not uncommon to drive 200 to 300 miles a day on this "search and destroy" mission. I would drive a while, then often I would stop my vehicle and get out and listen for shots or other activity. One afternoon while I was standing outside of my truck, I heard the distinct crack of a large caliber centerfire rifle. The entire southern portion of Michigan was closed to deer hunting with centerfire rifles. Crack, crack, again I heard rifle shots and pinpointed about where I thought the shots were coming from. The area was near the Detroit Edison Greenwood power plant property. As I was driving toward the area in question, I received a phone call from a hunter who had just been threatened by a foreign trespasser dressed in full camouflage who was carrying an AK-47 assault rifle. The trespassing incident happened to be taking place in the same mile section of land that I believed the rifle shots were coming from.

I soon began planning a long walk into the area composed of woodlots and farm fields. I know that conservation officers are supposed to wear a hat or vest of hunter orange color for safety reasons while afield during firearm deer season. But, I needed to sneak around undetected in stealth mode to try to catch the subjects red handed. I did not want to chase them off by me being seen from a long distance. I was also fighting the coming of nightfall. I knew that once darkness came, it would be much more difficult to find all of the men. I had about two hours of daylight left.

So, (stupid as it was) or (fun as it was) I decided to go searching for the subjects alone. I grabbed my issued .308 Springfield M1A assault rifle, took two 20 round magazines and off I went on a mission. I walked and walked, scanning the fields, brush, fence rows and woods for the subjects. I then found the subjects white pickup truck. Checking the truck, I spotted several boxes of .300 Magnum and 30-06 rifle cartridges, and could see six empty gun cases. There was a lot of deer blood scattered around the ground and on the truck. There was also a Point Blank brand bullet proof vest in plain view inside the truck. The stakes were getting higher by the minute. I called St. Clair County Sheriff Department dispatch and advised them of the situation of multiple rifles, trespassing, threats, and possession of body armor. Dispatch also advised me that the truck was owned by a subject with misdemeanor and felony warrants. I then heard many police units answering the call on the radio. St. Clair County Sheriff Deputies, Michigan State Police, Michigan DNR, and U.S. Border Patrol were all responding to my location. But we had a problem. I feared that if a bunch of police cars came rolling into the area, that the bad guys would either run or possibly shoot the officers as they approached in marked units and dressed in police uniforms.

The author next to a U.S. Border Patrol car with some of the weapons taken from a gang of illegal immigrants who were out poaching.

So again, I made the (dumb) (smart) (fun) decision to go it on my own. I called dispatch and advised them that I thought that it was too dangerous (for the backup officers) to respond into the area that I was in. I requested that the backup units stage about one-half mile away in two different directions and be at the ready for when I needed quick assistance. I continued walk hunting for the errant hunters. Now only one hour before dark, I began to worry. Could I catch them before nightfall? Then, as I was quietly walking along some brush and tall grass bordering a freshly cut corn field, I walked right up to two of the poachers. Right there, only 20 feet in front of me was quite a sight.

The two men were dressed in full camouflage and lying in the prone position, both facing away from me. They were both aiming scoped rifles and one of the rifles was mounted on a bipod. The scene looked like something out of a war movie instead of something one would see during deer hunting season. I quietly snuck up behind the suspects and when I was right behind them, I drew my .40 caliber Sig Sauer semi-automatic pistol. I then gave them orders, "Don't move, police, don't move, conservation officer, you are under arrest". I took their rifles from them after a brief struggle and then handcuffed them both. The rifle mounted on the bipod was a .300 Winchester Magnum. On the rifle was written "John Platzer Sniper Edition". Sweet, along with the foreign guys having warrants, they had bulletproof vests, we're poaching deer, and we're using a bona fide sniper rifle! Boy, was I into it deeply!

I called dispatch and advised them that I had two of the poachers in custody. When I looked around again, I could see three more camouflage rifle toting figures walking directly toward my location. I could see that the men in camo all had scoped rifles and were about 150 yards away from me. I was already within easy rifle range so I knew I had to do something quickly. God looked out for me once again, for when I glanced around, I saw a single large hickory tree only ten feet to my left. It was the only tree within 100 yards and it was right where I needed it for something to give me cover and concealment as the suspects approached. I told the two handcuffed men to shut up and not to say a word. I then took my position behind my new favorite hardwood tree. The three screwed poachers were still walking toward me, 50 yards away, then 40 yards away. The men closed the distance between us. I readied my .308 to make it a fair fight if it came down to that. One against three with two more near my feet. Almost fair. When the three approaching poachers were about 15 feet away from me, I ordered them to stop. I yelled out, "Stop, police, drop your guns". No response. I again yelled, "Drop your guns". Still no response. I had to yell "shut up" to the two subjects handcuffed on the ground, who were yelling in some foreign language to their friends. A very tense few moments indeed. If the two on the ground rushed me...and at the same time the three only 15 feet away started shooting at me...well, I might have had a problem and possibly one of my brothers would have had to write this story about how I went down. After more commands from the man (me) behind the big hickory tree who had 20 rounds of .308 ready to work, the three men dropped their guns. I ordered the three down to the ground and for a split second, I admired the scene. There, on the ground, were five foreign-looking men dressed in full camo, with five high powered rifles lying amongst them—all only feet in front of me. I called dispatch and asked for the backup officers to respond in to my location. Respond they did! Multiple agencies sent multiple cars, SUVs, and trucks. When border patrol heard that I had several foreign subjects with warrants and rifles, they sent three of their cars. Soon I had lots of help and the scene was secure. A sixth member of the group walked up to us and surrendered. He actually had a shotgun, was a US citizen, and had a license (surprise).

Five of the six hunters were found out to be illegally in the United States. They were not even American citizens, yet were breaking so many of our American laws. A list of some of the charges include:

- Five subjects were illegal aliens
- Six were dressed in full camouflage- (contrary to Michigan law requiring hunter orange safety clothing).
- Five were illegal aliens possessing weapons.
- Five possessed no hunting license of any kind.
- Four were trespassing.
- Two deer were killed illegally.
- Two had misdemeanor and felony warrants.
- Three attempted to kill turkey out of season.
- One threatened a legal hunter.
- Several had littered all around their vehicle.
- They possessed body armor during the commission of a crime.
- Five were using centerfire rifles in a shotgun only zone.

All in all, the poachers were charged with over 40 violations. All of the weapons were seized and five of the six men were taken away by the border patrol for detention and jailed on several felony charges.

In police work and in court proceedings, there is a general rule called the "fruit of the poisonous tree". In short, what this rule stands for is that if an officer does not follow established law or does something illegal, then anything the officer sees or finds from that point on is inadmissible as evidence. So, any evidence subsequent to an illegal act or search is therefore poisoned, and is bad evidence. Similarly, illegal immigrants written about in the story can be viewed the same way.

Since five of the six men broke customs and immigration laws and snuck into our country illegally, they were criminals to start with. They did not belong here enjoying our beautiful natural resources in the first place. They somehow got high powered rifles. Then they hunted our game animals without even buying hunting licenses, and intentionally broke many of our game laws. The blatant disregard for our laws was evident all the way from the beginning. First the illegal status, then to threatening legal hunters, trespassing on land owned legally by our tax paying citizens, killing animals which are protected and regulated through revenue collected from fishing and hunting license sales and from taxes. They were wrong and illegal from the beginning to the end.

I am real proud and honored to have been the officer that was able to stop the illegal insanity of these criminals. The day after I arrested these men, I was working and went into a small country store called the Fargo market. The owners are great people and are the real Americans who cling to their family, guns, religion, and hunting. They told me that they were glad that I was alright and that they heard that I went Rambo style by myself into the woods and took down the illegal immigrant poachers. I said thanks and yes, and that it is partly because of all the good people like them that I work so hard and risk so much for. And yes I told them if I had a chance to do it all again, I would go Rambo style and handle the situation the same way.

Big Fish Story

This situation began in early June one year when I arrested a sturgeon poacher. I confiscated a five-foot long sturgeon which had been dead for awhile and was already starting to smell bad. It was a warm spring night, and by the morning, the large prehistoric looking fish that lay dead in the bed of my black Chevy patrol truck was smelling dreadful. It was definitely past the point of human consumption.

I talked with my sergeant about the foul smelling large fish and about what to do with it, and how to dispose of it. He said to take a lot of pictures and put it out in the woods in the state game area. I decided against that idea because I did not want a bunch of phone calls from citizens about an enormous poached fish. Then, I remembered that I knew a guy in Sanilac County who had over 100 acres of land and loved to garden. I could not think of a better use than to return the fish back to nature to help fertilize a vegetable garden.

So, I called the landowner and asked him if he could cut up the evidence fish and bury it in his garden. I took the big fish to the man's house. With the gardener happy to have the fertilizer and also impressed with the size of the fish, I drove away knowing that the smelly evidence would be disposed of properly. Oh, boy was I wrong about that.

You see several hours later, the landowner's wife called me in a panic, stating that two DNR trucks just swooped in and the officers arrested her husband for poaching a sturgeon. "What?" I said. "Slow down. I don't understand what you are telling me." Then she gave me the details. Her husband loved his grandson and decided to pretend his grandson caught the big fish in his backyard pond, so his grandson could impress his friends at school. He hooked a hook in the fish's mouth and had his grandson reel in the now long dead fish. THEN he called a taxidermist and asked to have the surgeon mounted for his grandson! Knowing that sturgeon season was closed, the conscientious taxidermist called the DNR. Oh yeah, sturgeon don't even live in backyard ponds, so the taxidermist must have thought the story was a little fishy. The landowner had hidden the fish in a friend's freezer. The conservation officers instructed the man to show them the fish.

Knowing that there was no violation involved (only stupidity), I responded to their location. When I pulled into the "suspect's" friend's driveway, I could see two DNR trucks. The suspect was sitting in one of the patrol trucks. He had his arms folded over his chest. I heard him emphatically tell the interviewing officers, "Yup, my grandson caught that sturgeon in my pond, I swear on my mother's grave," (remember sturgeon don't even live in ponds). I said, "Shut up and quit lying, that fish came from me, it's evidence, and it is stinking and rotting. Now tell the truth."

Finally, with tears running down the man face, he admitted that I had given him the fish for disposal in his garden. Then, in another way of proving his love for his grandson, he told the officers that his grandson really did reel it in from the pond. I guess he did in a way. Wow, another roller coaster of emotions. The poor conservation officers thought that they had a great case. The taxidermist thought that he might get thousands of dollars of reward money. The homeowner thought that his grandson would be able to show off his trophy fish for years to come, and all I could think was that some people let their emotions interfere with their better judgment.

Songbird Slaughter

Many of us love to see songbirds. Many of us spend a lot of money on birdseed each year. Feeding birds is almost a tradition here in Michigan and in many states. So many people buy special blends of seed and suet and get a lot of enjoyment from just watching the birds.

Law protects all songbirds, except for Starlings and English Sparrows. Songbirds may not be hunted or killed. Yes, I know most kids walk around with BB guns shooting cans and occasionally shooting at birds when they are young. This story is not about some 12-year-old kid with his first BB gun out learning how to shoot. It is about an adult killing a lot of songbirds.

Many of my cases were made without getting a complaint or receiving citizen tips. Some cases were made by calls from concerned citizens, nature lovers, or irate neighbors.

One such irate lady called one day to advise me that her neighbor was shooting songbirds, all the time. She said that he would spend hours shooting out of the back window of his garage and that all of the birds in the area were disappearing. She was very upset and angry and felt bad for the birds. She was also upset that her family and the other neighbors were not able to enjoy seeing any birds at their bird feeders.

I responded and found the suspect, in a room in the rear of the garage. He had a high-powered pellet gun and had an open window facing the backyard. Quiet and respectful, the suspect answered, "Oh just shooting things," when I asked him what he was doing. "I see, did you shoot any birds?" I asked. "Just a couple," he said. I asked if I could look in his backyard for dead birds and he said that I could. I called for a backup car after I checked the suspect's record, and discovered he was a convicted felon and there was an officer safety caution issued for this residence.

My backup officer was St. Clair County Deputy Marty Stoyan. We checked all over the backyard. The suspect had filled large baking pans and cookie sheets with birdseed and then would shoot the birds when they came to eat. We found dead Cardinals, Robins, Orioles, Chickadees, Mourning Doves, Meadowlarks, and Blue Birds lying dead everywhere. Dozens and dozens of songbirds littered the yard.

I asked why he was shooting these pretty little harmless birds and he said that he just liked to kill things. I finished collecting evidence and concluded with the arrest. The fine for killing protected non-game birds is a hefty $100 for each one killed and I found over 50 of them! Oh yeah, I forgot to mention that the bird killer was a convicted sex offender living right by a school. People on the sex offender list are prohibited from living within 1,000 feet of a school. Several studies have shown a correlation between sex offenders and cruelty to animals and thrill killing. Based on this case of the pervert killing songbirds for no reason, I concur with the studies.

Stolen Van

High-speed chases. The day will come when criminal chases will no longer occur. There will eventually be some sort of electronic shut off device, blow up device, or netting device that will end the chase as soon as it begins. Something has to be done. Many innocent civilians and police officers are killed or injured each year in America during these chases. Myself, like all officers, feel so bad for the innocent victims and their suffering and mourning families and friends. Those of us who wear the badge know the sorrow, guilt and hurt that is possible each time we engage in a pursuit. Some agencies have a "no pursuit policy," others have very restrictive pursuit policies and rules.

Why is it the police officer's fault when some idiot elects to flee from the police? Who chose to start the ever so dangerous situation? I have never been in a police chase. I have never chased a police car. I have chased lots of criminals but never the police. So I ask, why is it called a police chase? No one is chasing the police.

Back only a few years, a criminal chase was classified as only a misdemeanor. Fortunately, someone convicted of fleeing from the police now faces a felony. Well, that's not good enough punishment for the thoughtless, brainless person who places the officers and the public in grave danger by fleeing in the first place.

So dangerous, so devastating, so destructive, so harmful, are only a few names to call these chases. As horrible as the consequences of these chases are, police cannot just quit and watch criminals speed away. What kind of lawless society would we have if every criminal could just drive away from the police and not get caught? Where is the justice in only arresting people who willfully stop to get arrested? I believe that the pursuit of fleeing criminals in motor vehicles is still a necessity. Police are well trained in pursuit driving and are even using stopping techniques such as stop spike strips and the pit maneuver technique to end car chases.

The result of chasing and catching a fleeing felon in a vehicle in a SAFE manner is and should always be our top priority when engaging in pursuits.

With all this said, most law enforcement officers really enjoy and look forward to being in police chases. It's the ultimate adrenaline rush. Why do people like to watch "Cops", where they show vehicle pursuits, or why are there television shows like "World's Scariest Police Chases"? What about car chase scenes in movies? The audience even feels the excitement. The controlled speeding, squealing tires, hard cornering, and white knuckle driving while in a marked police unit with lights and siren blaring is one of the most intense and breathtaking parts of police work.

Speaking of car chases, one afternoon, I was near the Blue Water Bridge along the St. Clair River when the Sheriff Department put out a BOL for a brown full-size van. The van had just been stolen from a party store parking lot by three thugs who fought with the van owner and cut his hand and left him bleeding as they drove away with his vehicle. Being only a few miles away from the store left me in a prime position to search for the brown van. Then, I spotted the brown van. I checked the license plate and it matched the one that was just stolen. I tried to keep up with the speeding van as I radioed to the other units that I had spotted the van. The van was on I-94 now and was accelerating away from me. For safety reasons, I had to engage my siren and flashers and contrary to standard practices tried to stop the fleeing felons myself. The driver and both passengers looked at me, laughed, and then sped up. The chase was on!

I called dispatch and advised them of my location and that we were westbound on I-94. Unfortunately for the Detroit-bound criminals, I-94 would soon pass through several police jurisdictions and small towns while traversing through three counties. Soon, St. Clair County Sheriff cars, Michigan State Police, and Port Huron Police cars joined the chase. Then, police units from agencies all the way from Marysville, St. Clair, to Chesterfield Township joined the chase. Altogether, we had over 20 police cars with lights and sirens on headed westbound on I-94. After 30 miles of this high-speed chase, after endangering police officers' and public lives, the subject driving the brown van tried to avoid spike strips set up in front of them. However, the van ran over the spikes with the two passenger side tires. Soon, the van hit a road sign, then came skidding to a stop. Immediately, the van doors opened, and all three idiots ran out. The vehicle chase now turned into a foot chase. Bursting out of our police cars, several officers began chasing the suspects. One of the subjects stopped, then ran back to the van and was placed under arrest. We chased the other two, then tackled both of them. A Chesterfield Township Officer and I got to take the driver down. He kept resisting. He told us that if he could have made it to Detroit that we would not chase him any longer, wrong. He told us that we were slow runners, wrong. He called us all sorts of racist things and continued with his verbal assaults as we kept him pinned to the ground. We then handcuffed the disorderly thief. It would have been real easy to engage the fool in a yelling match, but we kept professional and walked him (with the other handcuffed suspect) back to the large waiting fleet of police cars. Only another police officer would know what it feels like to walk a handcuffed criminal back to all the waiting police officers' cars. Only a criminal would know what it feels like to walk the "walk of shame" while handcuffed.

It's a pride thing. We were very proud of the fact that we were able to catch the criminals all the while with no one getting hurt, except for the suspects' pride.

One Ore in the Water

Marine safety patrols became even more important and common as the years went by. We had a statewide priority to spend many hours patrolling the lakes and rivers of Michigan. The state of Michigan even received federal funding to pay for boats, gas, oil, and wages. Many lives are saved each year by officers and deputies while on marine patrol. The theory is that the more time officers can spend patrolling in boats, the more of an impact they can have on keeping the public safe.

Marine safety funding became a large part of the DNR's budget. State and federal monies helped pay the wages of hundreds of conservation officers, many who worked over 300 to 400 hours a year on marine patrol. State and federal dollars were even used to purchase new patrol boats. The state-owned several older boats that were assigned to officers along with several new boats. One of the used boats happened to be a 20-foot Seacraft with a 200 horsepower Mercury motor on it. The boat had been assigned to my partner Jerry Prone for years. When Jerry retired, I asked if I could adopt his boat for me to use on patrol. The white fiberglass center console boat was a real pleasure to work from. Most days and nights I could even handle the boat by myself as I rescued people, towed people, and protected our fish resources.

On one hot summer night, I met one of my partners, Ken Kovach at 10:00 p.m. to begin a night patrol on the St. Clair River and lower Lake Huron. The black Mercury 200 horsepower motor started right up and we were off. We were wearing our float coats and rode away at 50 miles per hour under the Blue Water Bridge and we were really enjoying the night. After checking a few boats in Lower Lake Huron, we decided to travel south in the St. Clair River toward Marysville and St. Clair.

The Seacraft was a very seaworthy vessel. It had to be to withstand the untamed waters of the St. Clair River. In same spots, the river is over one mile wide and has depth of over 60 feet, and a southern flowing current of almost 10 knots. Add in the wind, boat wakes, and the continuous freighter traffic, and the river could be very dangerous and unforgiving place to work. I have personally seen many lives lost to the waters of the St. Clair River.

Anyway, as we were motoring along in my trustworthy 20-foot boat, we passed right next to the *Walter McCarty*, a 1000-foot Great Lakes freighter, and we also saw one of the ocean freighters that traveled all the way from Poland. The sights, sounds, and smells of the summer night surrounded us, but the danger of the waters and of the large vessels were always present in our minds.

Now being around midnight, we were traveling southbound just north of Marysville when something happened to our faithful Seacraft's Mercury motor. The motor caught on fire. What? On fire, you may ask. Yes. Smoke and flames started shooting out from our boat motor.

That's alright; we had plenty of water to put the fire out. Not too comforting, considering the fast current and the fact that we were now stranded in international waters in the middle of the river in a depth of over 40 feet. Add to the predicament was the fact that we were in the shipping channel. Those large, steel freighters would take almost one mile to come to a stop, and that is if they even saw us.

Panic almost set in. We laughed a little. We put the boat motor fire out with our fire extinguisher. Then I grabbed one of our two wooden emergency paddles. When I went to row with the paddle to try to push us toward shore hundreds of feet away, the wood paddle broke in half. Great, now we were up a creek (monster river) with only one paddle. It wasn't that bad, though. We only had a motor on fire, a broken paddle, and we were in the middle of a dangerous river at night with a 1000-foot steel freighter weighing over 100,000 tons bearing down on us.

We called St. Clair County Dispatch and advised them of our situation. We then used the broken paddle, the other old paddle, our hands to try to get out of the way of an oncoming giant vessel. We were flashing spotlights, flashlights, and yelling to alert other boaters of our pathetic situation. Real soon, we could see the blue flashes of a SCCSD marine boat coming to save us. My friends Bob Wright and Arnie Chickenowski (SCCSD deputies), attached a line to us and towed us to safety, then towed us all the way back to Port Huron.

A little scary, a little funny, and a little embarrassing night came to an end. Thanks again to the SCCSD Marine Division for helping us. The following year I did get a brand new 20-foot fiberglass Seapro boat with a 150 horsepower Mercury motor on it and the marine patrols continued.

2000 Pound Corn Pile

Conservation officers hear many excuses from poachers when they are caught. I have heard so many excuses over the years such as: "I thought the deer was a squirrel", "I saw movement", "I needed the meat," "I can't afford a license," "My wife told me to get some venison," "I did not know when season opens," and so on.

Pathetic excuses are a defense mechanism people use when they get caught. Instead of just admitting that they are poachers, these people usually make up sorry excuses in an attempt to make officers think that they really are not poachers. Here is a story about a poacher who told me all sorts of lies and excuses, maybe for his own benefit because I sure did not believe his bull.

While I was patrolling one beautiful October evening, a bow hunter friend of mine called me and advised me that he heard a rifle shot in the woods next to his property. It was bow season, and there was only about one hour of daylight left (you know, the time of night when the woods seem to come alive). I responded and walked to the area that the hunter pointed out to me. As I snuck up on the suspect's blind, I could see a guy sitting in the blind hunting. In front of the blind, was a 2,000-pound corn pile. Right there, laying dead on the excessive bait pile was a big eight point buck.

As dark settled in, the subject exited his blind carrying a scoped rifle and a compound bow. He walked back to his truck and backed his truck up to the bait pile. He then hooked a yellow tow strap up to the ungutted eight-point buck and tried to pull the buck into the truck bed using the tow strap to help. Several attempts to load the heavy buck failed. I began laughing as the poacher began getting tired. The poacher then hooked the tow strap to the bumper hitch of his truck and started dragging the buck through the woods and fields with his lights off. I ran up to the poacher's door and shined a flashlight on him, then on me to show him his worst nightmare, me. The subject told me that he had shot the buck with his bow and arrow. Wrong answer. After a while, the (finally) cooperative and confessing subject gave me the gory details of how he killed the buck illegally with his 30-06 rifle. The subject then gave me a written statement which included such excuses as, he needed the meat, is on workers' compensation, and has no money (except for bait).

Let's break down the excuses. He had no money and needed the meat. The poacher drove a brand new Ford pickup truck. The poacher spent a lot of money on buying over 2,000 pounds of shelled corn that he placed in the spot where he killed the eight-point buck. He also passed up several does and fawns while waiting for a buck. I think he would have just shot a doe if he really needed the meat. Then, he said he was on disability. When people are on disability or workers' compensation, they get a paycheck. Secondly, this man was healthy enough to climb into his tree blind and healthy enough to carry a lot of corn to his bait pile. Even though I showed compassion for the starving, injured, destitute man, I told him that I did not believe his excuses.

So then the real reason for killing the big buck came out. The poacher told me that he wanted to get the big buck before his neighbors did (now that's believable). Oh my, so many excuses, so little time, but for me another good illegal deer case.

I Got Struck by Lightning

The odds of getting struck by lightning are similar to the odds of winning the lottery. In a given year, the odds of a person getting struck are 1 in 700,000.

When I speak to hunting and fishing clubs, schools and colleges, and attend other speaking engagements I usually tell the group about my career. I talk about my love for the job, how I enjoy the interactions with the public and how I love protecting our natural resources. I tell the groups how my career has been golden, that I have seen it all and have done it all. I tell them that I have made so many poaching cases, have had so many chases, felony arrests, been involved in so many dangerous situations, and always seem to be at the right place at the right time. I even tell about getting struck by lightning when I was working one day. "What, you got hit by lightning, and you are still here?" they ask. I just smile and say "Yes, I am still here," in spite of the lightning and many other close calls. Yes, being a conservation officer carries significant risks, but the risks don't outweigh the rewards. I loved every minute of my patrols.

One dangerous situation occurred on a hot summer day. I spent a lot of time checking my state game area for litter and land abuse issues. On this one particular day, I could see ominous dark clouds approaching St. Clair County from the west. As I drove around the game area, I followed an old pickup truck that was loaded with what looked like an old refrigerator and an oven in the bed of the truck. The truck pulled off the gravel road and backed into a small parking area. I had to hide my patrol truck so the subjects would not be scared off. I then walked back to the area where the truck was backed into and hid and waited to see if they were going to throw the old appliances out into the state land. As I watched, the haunting dark clouds came closer and closer, and I could hear the roar of the thunder quickly approaching.

First lightning, then thunder, then seconds later another repeat, only closer. I looked around and thought about running toward my vehicle, but my desire to arrest someone littering was greater than my common sense to leave. Then BANG about 12 to 15 feet away to the east, a monster lightning bolt came crashing down and I immediately felt a blow to my chest. Some of the lightning found me! The lightning came through my ballistic metal plate in my body armor, and unknown to me exited through my femoral artery in my right thigh. Wow, loud, scary, intense, but still fascinating were some of the thoughts going through my mind. Even though my chest hurt right in the center of my breastbone, I kept waiting for the people to litter. Soon to my surprise, the truck left and I walked back to my patrol truck.

I continued working for a few hours, then wised up and decided to go to the hospital to be checked on. When I walked into the emergency room in uniform, the nurses thought I was on official business. When I told them I had been hit by lightning, they panicked, and hurried me into a room and had a doctor attend to me within minutes. Fearing serious damage, the doctor checked me out and said that I should be thankful that I remarkably showed no visible signs of injury or damage, only a sore chest. Later that night, I noticed a bruise on my right thigh, but otherwise, I felt fine.

Almost eight months later, my right calf hurt quite badly and was quite swollen. I went to the hospital where my sister Kristin worked on the heart surgery ultrasound team. We made small talk as my sister began the ultrasound on my leg. As she continued, she began to get teared up and told me that my leg was full of blood clots, and that my right leg's femoral artery had a hole in it! Oh great, I thought as I remembered the bruise on my right thigh in the same spot. The lightning exited through my femoral artery! Panic set in with doctors, nurses and specialists caring for me and there were some tense and scary moments during my four-day hospital stay. Soon I was home and eventually went back to work.

Boy, it sure felt good the first time I had a subject flee from me. I was able to run him down like a dog and was pleased that in spite of the lightning and blood clots I could still catch anyone I wanted. I could have gone on medical leave or disability leave, but I had too much pride, and I was having too much fun catching poachers and criminals, so I just tolerated any pain that I had and continued working.

In the Doghouse

In life and police work, building a good reputation and living off of that reputation pays huge dividends. I have had guys tell me, "I would have poached that big buck, but I know you are always around John." I have heard some guys say that they were going to run from me but heard that I enjoy running people down when they flee from me. I have heard that guys thought about fighting with me when I caught them but heard that I jacked up a friend of theirs. I have also heard that I am a really nice guy, but don't lie to me and don't mess with me. Matter of fact I heard it from the suspect in this story.

The winter snow had just melted away one early April day when the SCCSD received a call of a subject who shot a large turkey at a bird feeder in the Ruby area. Turkey season was still weeks away, and the prized birds were easy prey when feeding at places like bird feeders. Deputy Bob Gross responded to the location and was able to find the wadding from a 12 gauge shotgun shell, turkey feathers, and blood under a bird feeder. There was no dead turkey to be found, however.

Deputy Gross located the subject and questioned him for a period with the suspect not giving in at all. "No, no, I did not do it, there is no turkey, I know nothing," was all the subject kept saying. Then in front of the suspect, the deputy called his dispatch and asked to contact DNR Officer Borkovich. The 6'5" poacher overheard my radio traffic that I was en route to the turkey poaching location. He immediately said, "Oh, Borkovich is coming, I am in the doghouse now. My friends all told me that Borkovich is a real nice guy, but not to lie to him. Lying to Borkovich is not a good thing. When he gets here, I will tell him the truth." I arrived on location and then walked up to where the deputy and suspect were standing near the bird feeder. "Hi, I shot the turkey. I heard you are coming and I heard you are a real nice guy, but I was told not to lie to you. The turkey is a monster gobbler with a 15-inch beard," the suspect said. To those of us that turkey hunt, legally shooting a turkey with a 15-inch beard is like shooting a 10 or 12 point trophy buck. Yes, I was mad, but I acted calmly because we still did not know where the poached turkey was. We had a long conversation where the violator confessed to killing the trophy bird then driving it about 15 miles away and hiding it in a dog house behind his dad's house. See, the poacher was not the only one in the doghouse.

We drove to his dad's, and wrapped up in a blue tarp, hidden inside a doghouse in the backyard was the big bird. Without the cooperation of the turkey shooter, I would never have found the giant gobbler, and there would have been yet another record book trophy in the record books. Guess it pays to have a reputation out there.

Stolen Stop Signs

Hunting human beings is a challenge. Most humans are intelligent, educated, and have some common sense. By being wise and worldly, some people are difficult to catch when they break the law.

As smart and educated as people are, they still make mistakes and leave clues as they break the law. Humans also are creatures of habit, and many criminals get caught due to their predictable habits. One involuntary habit helped one of my great sergeants and I make a really strange case one night.

One night, my friend and sergeant, Jeff Pendergraff and I, were hunting for deer poachers. We would follow suspicious vehicles as they aimlessly drove slowly around on the country roads. We began following one particular car at about midnight. As I mentioned, people do certain things out of habit. One of the signals of wrongdoing was when the driver of the vehicle repeatedly hits his brakes. When people are involved in poaching or criminal activities, they can't seem to focus on more than one thing at a time. For example, when people are shining deer, they can't seem to just look for deer. They hit their brakes real often. This frequent braking is what got our attention focused on this car in the first place. As we followed the car for a long distance, the driver kept hitting the brakes, and then slowly would keep driving. Then every mile, the car would come to a complete stop for a few minutes.

Sergeant Pendergraff (later Captain Pendergraff) and I kept following the suspect vehicle, waiting to see a spotlight or hear a shot coming from the car. But the spotlight never shined, and the shots never rang out. After following the subjects (without our lights on), we decided to get a little closer to see what they were up to. When we got close enough to really watch the young men in the car, we saw them stop at an intersection and three of the guys got out of their car. Darn, they are not poaching, we commented to each other.

They were just stealing stop signs. What? Just stealing stop signs!

We actually watched the fools use wrenches to take the stop sign off of the green metal post. They then threw the stop sign into their trunk. They then took off toward the next sign. We drove through the intersection (since there was no stop sign) and pulled the car over. To our amazement, the entire trunk of the suspects' car was full of stop signs and yield signs.

Disappointed as we were that the suspects we caught were not poaching, we began piecing together the stop sign case. Then it hit us. These idiots not only were stealing hundreds and hundreds of dollars worth of signs, they were placing the public's lives and safety in jeopardy. So many intersections were left unmarked and unprotected by the sign thefts. Innocent people could have been killed by being hit in broadside collisions at the intersections.

Very scary indeed, how much we take for granted that the other guy is going to see a stop sign and stop. Broadside collisions happen all too often due to drunk drivers, distracted driving, and careless drivers. Imagine how many more accidents would occur at intersections without stop signs at all.

Anyway, we did respond back to the suspects' homes and confiscated several more signs that they had stolen earlier. What could they have been thinking? Theft is one thing, but when someone steals something like a stop sign, the severity of the theft really escalates. Fortunately, we caught these guys in the act and returned the signs to the road commission and they put all the signs back up to help keep our intersections a little safer.

Deer Hanging in April

Fine restaurants advertise "aged Black Angus Beef" and "aged grade A steaks." These expensive cuts of meat are usually more tender beef. Most hunters also know the value of aging their venison. Or in common language, by "letting their deer hang." Hunters have used buck poles for years. Buck poles are sometimes used for events such as big buck contests for bragging rights. But the main reason people use buck poles is for hanging deer and allowing the blood to drip from the carcass. This allows the muscle fiber in the meat a chance to age and breakdown.

So aging a deer is a normal and useful procedure. But over-aging a deer, well that's another story. Read on. One April evening, I responded to assist the St. Clair County Sheriff on a call where there was a smell of a dead body in a residence. The homeowner granted us permission to see inside his home. We walked inside and found the source of the smell. There, hanging in the kitchen was a skinned out deer. Okay, hanging in the kitchen may have been a little strange, but the deer had been hanging since the past November, for a full five months! The stench was so bad that I could barely breathe and I immediately got a stomach ache.

The homeowner had cut a hole in the kitchen ceiling and hooked a rope around the bottom cord of the roof truss. His deer had hung there, first dripping blood on the carpet, then through the months, had gone through several stages of decomposition. The carcass also underwent attacks from insects like flies and beetles, and through these pests' life cycles, there was a five-inch tall pile of dead worms, beetles, larvae, and other matter on the carpet under the deer. I've heard of aged beef and aged venison, but not for five months indoors and with flies and bugs all over the meat. I think the saying "too much of a good thing" might apply here..

Frozen Waterfowl

We have all seen rescue scenes where quick thinking people save people. We have also seen dogs, horses, or deer rescued after getting caught in flood waters or being rescued after falling through the ice. These heroic rescues and rescue attempts get a lot of attention when shown on the evening news. There are a lot of good people left in this sometimes crazy world that we live in. These good people show compassion and care to people and animals who are less fortunate. Compassionate people care for the helpless, young, feeble, old, and disabled, and those facing adverse circumstances from injuries, fires, and accidents. These caring people also care for pets and wild birds, fish, and animals. Many of us feel the pain of an innocent bird or animal when it is suffering and struggling.

To an avid hunter, "getting" an animal or bird is a thrill. The hours spent afield are relaxing, rewarding, and somehow renew one's spirit to be out enjoying nature. It is just a pleasure to be outside enjoying nature. Part of hunting also sometimes involves the taking, killing, bagging, or harvesting an animal or bird. The quick, humane "getting" of game is what hunters strive for. This great pastime has been passed down for generations.

Although many of us enjoy the hunt and the harvesting, many of us also have kind hearts and want to help or save birds and animals as often as we can. One such incident happened in February along the St. Clair River. Morning temperatures dropped to a minus 29 degrees Fahrenheit at the St. Clair County Airport on Sunday morning. Now it was Monday morning and still almost 20 degrees below zero. We were in a deep freeze. The Great Lakes were surveyed and determined to be 85% frozen! Many migrating ducks from the northern tier of North America had gathered in Lower Lake Huron and the St. Clair River but were quickly running out of open water. Canvasbacks, Redheads, Scaub, Old Squaw (Long Tails), and other cherished ducks were gathered by the thousands in the open areas near downtown Port Huron, feeding in the St. Clair River.

What a gorgeous sight. The winter plumage of the ducks made quite an impression on both waterfowl hunters and bird watchers alike. One day, my daughter Chelsea and I took binoculars and a camera and ventured to the river's edge to enjoy some of nature's beauty. But when we walked closer to the river, we saw some of nature's cruelest sights. There were dead ducks everywhere. Several of the ducks were still alive but frozen to the ice edges and ice shelves. A drake Canvasback kept jumping and struggling to free itself, but could not get free from the ice.

You see, the ducks were sitting on the ice, then the temperature dropped drastically. The thin layer of water on top of the ice would quickly freeze, attaching the bird's tail and underside feathers to the ice. Since the ducks' feathers are such good insulators from cold (you know, goose down, duck down), the birds did not feel the cold. Morning would come and unbeknownst to them, their feathers would be attached to the ice and they could not move to swim, fly, eat, or drink.

Seeing these poor, defenseless, suffering ducks bothered us. The hunter instincts (chasing, hunting, and shooting game type of feelings) were nowhere to be found. Instead, we felt compelled to do something to save the dying birds. We called everybody and anybody in hopes of getting some help, but we soon realized the rescue would fall on our compassionate shoulders. We rushed to get life jackets and warmer clothes and a 20 foot long aluminum pole. We briefly thought, why were we doing this? Why should we risk our safety? Because, these trapped, defenseless ducks were still some of God's creatures. Philosophically speaking, I believe we should take care of those who are unable to care for themselves and in our minds, this included taking care of wild birds and animals.

The first duck saved was a hen Redhead. We chipped away at the ice and had to pull out a couple of her feathers, then Chelsea wrapped the duck up in her (goose down coat and we took the hen to the van and warmed her up by the heater for almost an hour. The poor thing just stared at us, like she was trying to say thank you. A wild duck, who flew hundreds or possibly thousands of miles to get here, was just sitting there looking around. Soon, she began moving more, then got a little feisty, so we carried her back down to the river and released her. She swam around at first, then dove down in search of food. We did it. We saved one of the birds. One little buddy survived. Then more sadness, we discovered more dead ducks everywhere. We dug out several more live ducks. One female Old Squaw was so adorable as we held her by the heater that it was almost difficult to return her to

100

the wild. Several citizens and newspaper reporters from the Times Herald Newspaper thanked us for helping the stranded and suffering ducks.

Then we spotted two Bald Eagles hunting and chasing ducks along the river. We told the reporters that we could not get mad at the Bald Eagles for chasing and killing ducks because that was just part of nature. And yes, I know freezing to death is also part of nature, but it was something that did not need to happen if we could help it.

Braving the cold, and climbing down onto the frozen water was not the smartest thing that we had ever done, but surely one of the kindest and most rewarding things that we had done in awhile. As dumb as it was, we went back on several other days to help our little-feathered friends.

We Have a Live Wire Here, John

Loading gear into my patrol truck to head out for another evening of deer poacher hunting seemed a lot like packing for vacation. The anticipation was very similar to the feeling of going "up north" or somewhere fun. On this particular day, CO Jason Haines met me and we excitedly loaded our gear and planned our night of work. We checked several areas of St. Clair County. With no direct supervision telling us where to work or what to work on, we continued searching for miles and miles. We talked about our wives and kids, sports, guns, and hunting and fishing as we searched for bad guys. Some nights were slower than others. This night was one of the slow ones. We stopped a few vehicles and assisted the county on a traffic stop.

Then at about 11:30 p.m., while working near Emmett, we spotted a very slow moving vehicle driving aimlessly on the back roads. We blacked out and followed the vehicle without our headlights on. The vehicle would stop, then slowly drive around and after making three left turns, we pulled up close to the vehicle and then turned on our emergency lights. We then lit the driver up with our spotlights. The vehicle did not stop but instead continued southbound on the gravel road. Now with siren blaring and blue lights flashing, we kept after the vehicle. I reached for the radio and called St. Clair County Dispatch and said, "County, 9-1-3-4, we are in a chase".

But just then, the fleeing driver pulled into a driveway. As we pulled into the driveway behind the suspect's vehicle, the driver's door opened and the suspect jumped out and began running. As I quickly got out of the driver's side door I began running after the fleeing man and to my surprise, Jason had quickly gotten out and was running with me. I had never seen another officer get out so quickly. We started gaining on the suspect then we did a double tackle on the man as he ran around the side of his yellow house. Jason yelled, "We have a live wire here, John." I thought, yeah, he is still fighting us off. But then I found out why Jason said, "live wire".

ZAP! Then another ZAP, then ZAP! I felt the sting from an electric shock. Jason said "live wire" not because the suspect was flailing around but because we were getting zapped by the electricity from an electric fence. You see, the suspect had intentionally run us directly into an electric cattle fence, and we were getting shocked over and over as we fought with the man. We arrested him, then later laughed and talked about the incident and compared the residual shock feeling we both still felt as we drove home.

Homecoming Dance

There are a lot of country songs about girls. Girls in trucks, girls fishing, girls drinking whiskey, girls shooting guns, and country girls all muddy and sweaty wearing cutoffs or tight jeans or cowboy boots. But I've never heard one song about country girls getting sprayed by a skunk and then going to a dance all dressed up.

Another October was upon me. As I patrolled in search of deer poachers, I observed an ORV coming toward me on Brown Road in Greenwood Township. I turned my flashers on and stopped the four-wheeler from the head-on position on the gravel road. There, in front of me were two high school girls all dressed up for their homecoming dance. As I walked toward the girls, I immediately smelled the distinct odor of a skunk. I then noticed a rope tied to the four wheeler. This rope was attached to a Havahart™ live trap which contained a live skunk. What???

I tried not to laugh as the two country girls told me what they were doing. You see, their dad had a trap in their horse barn and caught the skunk, and he was going to kill it. So even though the dance was quickly approaching, the girls thought the skunk was really cute and while their dad was in the house, they decided to tow the trap down the road a couple of miles and let the skunk go. The sight of the dressed up girls and the spraying skunk being dragged on the road made me laugh. I told the girls to drive home carefully after letting the skunk go and to enjoy their dance. I laughed as I drove away, and I wondered if the dad would be mad. I also wondered how many boys at the prom would wonder why the girls smelled like skunk. Maybe the dad knew what he was doing after all. He might have figured that the skunk smell might have kept the boys at the dance from getting too close to his daughters.

Poachers Talking Bad Behind My Back

W hy must some people lie about police officers? Why do they add or delete details to make an officer look bad? Why do they talk behind officers' backs? In religious language, why do they bear false witness? Lying or embellishing information in an attempt to harm an officer is something that happens often and is not appreciated. Usually, officers do not even know who slandered them or made up a lie or started a rumor. Sometimes, as in this story, an officer finds out.

One night while I was hunting for deer poachers, I saw a truck coming out of some woods, and I pulled the truck over. Walking up to the pickup truck, I noticed three untagged does laying in the bed of the truck. I talked to the two occupants, who happened to be brothers. After some consideration, I only wrote one ticket for just one untagged deer. The brothers seemed polite, and I had never had problems with them in the past. I even let the subjects keep all three deer after they located their tags and put them on the deer. The subjects shook my hand and thanked me for giving them such a good deal.

Three days later, a friend of mine, Michigan State Police trooper Mike Powell, and I were goose hunting in the same vicinity where I had pulled over the truck with the untagged deer in it. After we had finished hunting, I walked back to get my truck. My trooper friend stood near the side of the road, waiting to load up our decoys. I looked back toward my hunting partner and saw a black pickup truck pull up next to him. I recognized the black pickup truck as the same truck that belonged to the two brothers who I had given such a good deal to just a few days earlier. When I drove up to begin loading our decoys, my trooper buddy told me that the subjects in the truck had talked real bad about me. They even mentioned me by name as they took their shots at me verbally and then they drove away. Interesting I thought, talking bad about me even though I had given them such a good deal only three days earlier. As fate would have it, only two weeks later I got a call from the two brothers. The unappreciative brothers asked me for a favor. They had wounded a six-point buck, and they had followed the blood trail to the edge of a privately owned section of property owned by the Detroit Edison Company. The property was posted with no hunting no trespassing signs, and the subjects had called me to ask me to help them retrieve their deer. I said sure; I like helping hunters. I looked down, saw the blood trail and we began tracking the deer. I let the two knuckleheads walk with me even though I made them leave their guns behind.

We made small talk as we followed the scant blood trail. They were so thankful that I was helping them. Then after about a half of a mile walk, once we were in the thickest, nastiest brush that I could find, I stopped and confronted the brothers. I told them that I had heard about how they were talking badly about me. I refreshed their short term memories by reminding them of the contact that they had had with the goose hunter from a couple of weeks earlier. Then I advised them that the hunter was a very credible witness. He worked for the Michigan State Police! I asked the foolish brothers how could they talk so badly behind my back, especially after how well I had treated them earlier.

Then I gave them this offer. "If you want to lie and talk bad behind my back, go ahead and say it to my face," I said. I then told them that there were no witnesses, except for the woods. I told the two brothers that since we were all alone and lacked witnesses, if they thought that they were tough guys and can go around making up lies about me, and I said, "Try lying about me now." I also told them that I would leave them right there for someone else to find. This was my way of handling the situation instead of trying to deal with the courts, lawyers, and possibly a slander lawsuit.

They stuttered and nervously apologized over and over and over and wanted no part of a confrontation. I laughed and told them to keep their big mouths shut. We never did find the deer and the day ended peacefully for them. To this day, I never had an issue with either one of the two brothers again. Matter of fact, they would wave and smile at me each time that I encountered them from that day forward. Maybe my way of handling the situation was a little unorthodox, but I sure got my point across.

Shark Bait

Sticks and stones may break my bones, but names will never hurt me. That all sounds nice and cute, but sometimes spoken words need to be taken seriously. Officers must have thick skin while dealing with the public. Minor threats, people swearing at us, and rude and insulting comments are just a few of the words that officers need to tune out. If an officer overreacted each time someone was rude, it would make for a frustrating, stressful, and dangerous work day. But, once in awhile, an officer needs to meet fire with fire, and realize that words could cause harm. That once in awhile happened one night while my volunteer conservation officer wife, Nancy, and I were patrolling.

I was checking smelt dippers (back when there were lots of smelt) along the edge of the fast moving waters of the St. Clair River. I was a newer officer, and I was walking at 11:30 p.m. with my wife. One of the intoxicated fishermen in a large group yelled out, "Here comes shark bait, let's throw them in." I was new and did not know anyone, and they did not know me or what kind of a guy that I was. I looked at the group, then looked toward the road and thankfully saw a Michigan State Police car driving by. I flashed my flashlight, signaling for assistance. Now, three of us against forty, the odds were slightly better.

I walked to the big mouthed subject and said, "Go ahead and try to throw me in" (the river is 30 feet deep with 10-knot current). The big mouth said, "Yeah, what would you do?" I replied, "I would shoot you before I died in that river." I stated, "If you try to kill me then I will kill you first." Then the whole group circled us, and someone said, "Are you serious? You would shoot us?" I again said that, "If I thought my life was in danger by being thrown into that fast, cold water, then yes, I would shoot you!" I then asked kindly, "Any more questions?" "Nope" and "sorry" was all I heard.

From that night forward for the next 24 years, I never had a threat or even heard a bad word from anyone on the entire boardwalk in Port Huron. I proved that I was not afraid of anyone. More importantly, over time, I proved that I treated the public fairly. I showed hunters and fishermen that I gave far more warnings than tickets, and I was always fair, polite, and compassionate when dealing with the public. I never had another bad incident along the river again. I was actually a welcomed sight along the St. Clair River and never needed to deal with any threats or words or sticks or stones. After all, most of the time outdoors people are just everyday good people just out enjoying nature. Fortunately for them and me, they figured out how I thought, worked, and how fairly I treated them.

Net Across Mill Creek

I walked a lot of miles while on patrol, sometimes walking four or five miles at a time while hunting for fish and game poachers. I would find amazing things far away from roads and witnesses.

One such walk occurred in October during my fall fish runs. Salmon would swim from Lake Huron up the Black River and continue up Mill Creek to the Brockway Area, then toward the Yale and Imlay City area. On this night, I began working in the dark along Mill Creek around 9:30 p.m. I saw a few salmon, and after about a mile of slowly searching, I heard voices ahead.

As I snuck up to see what the suspects were doing, I couldn't believe what I saw. There, right in front of me, were five men working a long net across Mill Creek. The huge net hung on a cable that stretched from bank to bank. The net looked just like the nets used on tennis courts. The net system they had blocking the creek was even about the same length as a tennis court net. I watched as the poachers used a large crank handle to haul in the net, then place the net back into Mill Creek-completely blocking the creek.

Periodically, they would use the crank to winch the net up and capture some of the salmon. I called for backup since there were five of them and only one of me. It was now 11:00 p.m. and I was one mile from any road.

Sergeant Jeff Pendergraff quietly walked to my location. We watched the poachers tending to the long net for a little while as we made our plan for attack. We jumped out at the poachers. We handcuffed the loud ones and began collecting evidence. Two of the salmon poachers even traveled all the way from Chicago. We could have waited all night to let the fish stealers gather more and more fish to rack up more fines, costs, and restitution to get more penalties (illegal salmon cost an additional $10.00 per pound per fish in restitution).) But that would not have been fair to the resource. These poachers worked very hard to carry in nets, cable, cranks and to willfully and intentionally violate our fishing laws. They seemed very surprised to have been caught way back in the woods! There were no foot chases, no fighting or resistance, just a look of shock on their faces of being found. I smiled and rejoiced in the fact that the good guys won again.

Your Tennis Shoes Are Too Big

A frantic call came into St. Clair County's dispatch one afternoon from the manager of my local Wal-Mart store. The angry, shook-up manager told the dispatcher that two males had stolen over $1,000.00 worth of cell phones and electronics from his store. The thieves then ran when confronted about the stolen items.

When the manager went outside, he got into his car and drove through his store's parking lot in an attempt to get the thieves' license plate. The manager spotted the suspects' car, but then the driver of the bad guys' car drove straight at the manager's car and crashed into his car head-on! With both vehicles disabled now, both criminals took off running on foot.

Being a priority call involving larceny and felonious assault, I responded emergency time as fast as I could, but the suspects were gone. I pulled up to the crash scene along with a county car. We first checked to make sure that the taxpaying, hard-working manager was not badly injured, then got the suspects' descriptions and began looking for the thugs.

After searching the area for awhile, we begin to wonder if the thugs may have fled the area. We started checking farther and farther from the crash scene. I headed over to check around a dumpster behind a Ruby Tuesday restaurant.

When I walked into the area inside of the wood privacy fence, I looked behind the dumpster, and I was face-to-face with the suspect. I rushed him and began placing the 30-year-old from Detroit in handcuffs. The fool began crying out for his mama. "Mama," I said, as I began laughing. Deputies Gill Sanchez, Gary Antilla, and Sergeant Joe Hernandez soon responded, and we placed the felon in deputy Sanchez's patrol car.

The second suspect was harder to find, even though his description should have made him easier to locate. He was described as being very tall, wearing a red jacket, and wearing giant, maybe size 17 or 18, bright blue tennis shoes. We looked and looked for the thief but began worrying that the suspect may have used a vehicle to elude us. Just for kicks, I decided to check every single parked car in a nearby car dealership lot. After checking dozens and dozens of cars and trucks without any luck, I walked up toward a very large, white Sprinter conversion van. Then I noticed something out of place. A giant bright blue tennis shoe was hanging down from the frame of the van. When I got closer, I looked under the van, and there he was, the second felon (he was using a vehicle to elude us after all). He had crawled up alongside the frame and axle and hidden himself in a crazy contorted position. The suspect had picked a large vehicle to hide under and had done a great job of hiding himself. He was hidden so well except for the fact that his shoes were too big. I held the suspect at gunpoint and called for backup. Deputy Sanchez, Deputy Antilla, and Sergeant Hernandez did respond and could not believe how well the criminal had hidden himself. We ordered the contortionist with shoes too big to come out, and then we placed him under arrest.

I had to bite my lip to keep me from saying something about the thief's large (expensive) bright blue tennis shoes. I just smiled and added two more notches to my gun belt (arrest total).

Oops, I Left a Dead Walleye
Under the Seat in the Chief's Car

Getting along well with the DNR chief of the law enforcement is always a good thing. Chief Herb Burns and I had such a good relationship that he would often come over to ride with me on patrol. On other nights we would head out and fish together.

On one June day, Chief Burns came over, and we decided that we would ride around in his silver unmarked patrol car. We had a nice day. We wrote a couple of tickets and then we encountered a subject with an undersized walleye. I educated the rookie angler about the reason for size limits, and then I gave him a warning instead of giving him a ticket. I seized the dead walleye from the fisherman, and we walked back to the chief's car. My intention was to give the fish to someone who needed it, so I put it underneath the passenger seat for safe keeping as we drove away.

For the next hour, Chief Burns and I talked about my contacts with the public that day. He kept mentioning to me that he appreciated my demeanor and attitude when dealing with the public. The chief told me that I had a kind and gentle way of dealing with the public and that treating the public good was a good thing for the Department of Natural Resources.

I was so pleased with all of the compliments that I had received from the chief that I forgot to take the fish from underneath the seat when I got dropped off at home later. Chief Burns then drove back to Lansing and being a Friday, parked his car for the weekend and then went home. The hot, humid June weather warmed up the fish for over two days and greeted the chief with a smelly surprise when he got in his car on Monday morning.

Two weeks later, Chief Burns and Assistant Chief Wayne Kangas came over for a night of working. Very calmly, Chief Burns asked me what had I done with the fish that I confiscated the last time that we had worked together. My jaw dropped when I realized what I had done. Of all the cars to leave the fish in for two and a half days, why did I pick the chief's car? I apologized and he didn't even get mad at me, and he must have believed my story that the leftover fish incident was an accident.

It's a good thing that I liked the Chief, because the hidden fish trick would be a really good thing to do to someone that I really did not like. Just kidding, maybe. 112

Elk antlers lead to machine guns

The author surveying some of the 54 newspaper boxes dumped into our rivers.

Author with trophy turkey that a poacher hid in this doghouse

Author with some of the sixty deer poached by one group

Two illegal deer hidden in a tree way back behind a residence

Deer illegally killed in Montana by a Michigan hunter. The author worked with Montana Fish and Game Department on this poaching case

Photo shows what happened when author was searching for this lost hunter

Author and his new boat the replaced his patrol boat that caught on fire

Author with illegal Sturgeon that suspects claimed "hid itself" in their boat

Author with the weapons used by a gang of poachers

Deer from story "Ultimate Life and Death"

One of the many trout speared one night by poachers near Lake Huron

14-point buck poached

Author with State Police assisting him on another illegal deer case

Photo shows author with one of the two big bucks poached during archery season

Author with some of the young geese killed by a home owner

Bad Timing Got Stuck

While patrolling in the Port Huron State Game Area late one August night, I noticed a single set of truck tracks that went around one of the DNR gates. The tracks passed right in front of a "No Motorized Vehicles" sign.

I followed the truck tracks past a pond and through a White Pine thicket. Maybe the occupants of the truck were just enjoying and appreciating the beauty of the state-owned land that belonged to all of us. Or maybe not. Up ahead of me, I could see the vehicle stuck and the occupants feverishly trying to push the truck out. I approached the truck and advised the subjects that I needed their driver's licenses, and that it was illegal to operate their vehicle inside the game area. I looked back behind the truck and observed an entire truck load of shingles, nails, and wood. The large litter pile was about 200 feet behind the truck. The truck tracks led straight from the pile of garbage to the stuck truck. And there was also some shingles and debris still in the bed of the truck.

The subjects did confess to littering, and I also arrested the driver for several outstanding warrants.

Just like the saying goes, if the dog wouldn't have stopped to take a...he would have caught the rabbit. In this case, if the ignorant litterers wouldn't have gotten stuck, they would have gotten away.

What would our state and federal forest land look like if conservation officers, federal wildlife officers and police officers were not patrolling them? Would they become one big eyesore of a junk pile or a landfill? Fortunately, many of us officers take pride in preserving our natural resources and have a real interest in protecting our forest land. For as many litter cases as officers make, there are still thoughtless people who have no regard for our resources and who get away with dumping litter.

Nobody Sneaks Up On Me

After years and years of quietly sneaking up on suspects, some officers get very good at working in sneak mode. I took a lot of pride in how I could almost float through the woods while watching people. I learned what to step on and what not to step on. I learned what weather was best for walking quietly. I would pick my route or path through the woods or along river edges. I wore L.L. Bean rubber soled Maine hunting boots on many occasions. Sometimes, I could get so close to the suspects that I could touch them. Usually, I would not touch them for fear that they might have a heart attack or something.

It does wonders for an officer's reputation when he or she sneaks up real close to a suspect. The word spreads amongst other hunters and fishermen when an officer can quickly and quietly approach people. Since an officer can't be in all places at one time, an officer needs a reputation that he or she might sneak up on a poacher at any time, day or night.

Rarefied air greeted us on this fine October day. Mitch Babcock, Chanie Turk, Ron McCarty and Mike Radamaker and I all met to discuss our plan to patrol for fish poachers. The salmon were in the river by the hundreds. Big beautiful Chinook salmon were concentrated in certain spawning areas of the river. After making our hunting plans for the day, we all split up and wandered off to our assigned areas to work.

I got dropped off near a bridge and was easily able to follow a well-worn path along the river's edge. I found a few beer cans, a smashed styrofoam cooler and a wad of 40-pound test monofilament line along the path but found no salmon fisherman. The further I walked away from the bridge, the worse the footpath got until I needed to follow a couple of sets of boot tracks, then eventually followed only faint signs of someone walking ahead of me. Then I heard splashing and voices not too far away. I quickly and quietly got closer to the area where I had heard the commotion. Then I saw one man reeling in a salmon that was snagged between the dorsal fin and the tail. Another man was chasing the huge salmon with a big landing net. The men and the salmon were making a lot of noise. It is when people are frantically trying to net salmon that they are easiest to sneak up on.

But then I caught movement between the two fish poachers and myself. It was the lookout man. The lookout man was pacing back and forth on the river bank behind his two poaching friends. I later found out that he was supposed to warn the other two guys if the DNR came. My dark green pants and gray uniform shirt must have blended in quite well because so far the lookout man was failing at his job. I had already seen the illegal fishing activity. But I wanted to get closer to the poachers to be able to see the exact type of snag hooks the subjects were using. I also needed to get close enough to prevent them from cutting the rope loose and losing the evidence.

So, I crept closer and closer to the lookout man. He was doing a fair job now, and I had to concentrate on my movements. I needed to walk through some thick underbrush and some downed trees to avoid being seen. The soft rubber soles on my boots helped me feel my way over branches and twigs. I could feel the branches under my feet, and before I would put my weight on them, I would quietly step aside to avoid snapping the twigs. Eventually, I got about three feet behind the lookout man, then I whispered, "Don't move, conservation officer, don't yell and don't move".

The lookout man spun around on me in some sort of Martial arts stance. He was in a fighting position, fists clenched, knees bent, and his center of gravity was real low, similar to how a cougar crouches before springing on prey. He began circling me in a very threatening way and then said, "Nobody sneaks up on me." (Oh I think I hurt his pride, poor baby).

The lookout man proceeded to tell me that he did not like anyone sneaking up on him. He told me that he had just gotten out of Jackson prison, and in prison, a man never lets anyone sneak up on him (hmm, maybe for a couple of reasons I thought). Still circling me and ready to strike, the lookout man sort of looked intimidating. So I began laughing at the paranoid "tough guy," I told him to go ahead and attack me, and I would make sure he went straight back to prison so he could watch his back some more. I told him that I would arrest him for assaulting a police officer. I then explained that even though I had hurt his feelings, I was not mad at him and would not arrest him, unless he tried to fight with me or warn his fisherman friends. I also calmly explained to him that more than his feelings would be hurt if he attacked me.

The lookout man became meek and quiet and just stood there as I began sneaking up on his two friends. Sure enough, when I got real close to the fishermen, they each used their lit cigarettes to burn their fishing line in half to get rid of their M-60 lead weighted snagging hooks. Too late for that I thought. There they stood, two stooges with 11 illegal salmon and all the while wondering why the third stooge did not do his job.

The two men were from Illinois. When I asked for their identification, both men reached into their left shirt pockets and handed me their drivers licenses, fishing licenses, and three crisp $100.00 bills. They explained to me that they keep the money with their licenses to use for bond money since they were non-residents of Michigan. Without bond money, anyone arrested needs to go to jail to assure that they would take care of their fines and costs. Funny, how these guys came so prepared, each carrying $300.00 cash and each relying on the lookout man to warn them when the conservation officer showed up. Their plan almost worked. The two snaggers got ticketed, and the lookout man probably has a sore neck from looking behind him all of the time.

You Are Bleeding, Did You Get Cut or Something?

It was opening morning of deer season, at about 9:30 a.m. when I drove up next to a hunter standing on the side of the road. The hunter waved at me and I could clearly see blood all over his hands, face, and body. The season had only been open for a couple of hours, but it was very logical to think that the hunter had gotten a deer. I asked him if he got a deer, and he said, "No."

"Oh, did you cut yourself or something?" I asked.

"Yes,"

I asked, "where."

The hunter said, "Ah, here, no there, no here," as he pointed to his face and hands searching for a cut.

I smiled and said, "Alright, I've known you for years, I like your whole family, but let's get this over with" and I asked him to show me his deer.

"Ok, John, I took them back to the house already."

Hmmm. We went to his house and we followed the bloody drag marks up the front steps, across the porch and through the foyer.

The hunter said, "There's my deer" as he pointed to two small bucks laying in a heap at the bottom of the bloody stairs. The five-point was already gutted and the six-point was not gutted at all.

The hunter was a likeable kid and was very polite and cooperative with me. He then told me that he did not even buy a hunting license. Knowing that his family really did need the meat (why he did not just shoot a doe for meat is another story), I made a deal with the hunter. I sent him up to the Fargo Market to buy his licenses and then I had him tag the bucks. I only gave him a ticket for having the untagged deer instead of arresting him for illegal deer killing. I also let him keep both deer to help feed his family.

Almost two years later, I found out that the same subject had been raising a fawn illegally. On one August day, I drove up near the subject's house to deal with the fawn issue. When I got close, I saw the same subject and he waved at me (just like before). I also saw blood all over his hands and body (just like before). So two years later, I asked him the same questions. "Did you get a deer or did you cut yourself or something?" Only this time the subject did not lie to me. He told me that he did not shoot a deer and he was right. He then explained how he got so much blood on himself.

The bleeding subject went on to describe how he raised an orphaned fawn and when the deer got bigger and stronger, the subject tackled the deer to try to take it back inside his house. But the young deer kicked the guy with its front hoof. Deer legs are strong, and their hooves are sharp. When the scared deer kicked the subject, its hoof sliced his left hand wide open. The poor guy had a deep gash, almost ½-inch deep across his hand.

I felt sorry for the subject in a way. Maybe he was really helping an orphaned fawn. He still should have called the authorities about the deer, though. Anyway, the deer looked healthy and ran into the woods. I did not even ticket the poor injured guy. I figured that the deer got enough revenge (for his dad and uncle) and was able to serve up a little poetic justice all by itself.

We Ain't Got No Deer

While I was out patrolling the back roads one deer season, I spotted an old jacked up Blazer "slow rolling" ahead of me. I followed the blazer as the occupants' road hunted the gravel roads right during the heart of deer season. The hunters' windows were down, and they were going at a very slow, barely moving speed as they scoured the fence rows and the woods for deer.

Eventually, I pulled the blazer over. As I walked up toward the vehicle, I noticed that the occupants were all moving around and throwing jackets and clothing all over inside of the truck. I walked up to the driver's window and told everybody to hold still and to show me their hands. I then looked into the truck and on the center console, I saw a deer heart with a large hunting knife sticking into it and into the console.

I politely asked, "Did you get a deer today?" "No," was the answer I received. "Did you get a deer yesterday? How about all season?" "No, no one got any deer." I then asked, "Do you have any deer in this vehicle?" They responded with, "No, we haven't even seen any deer. We ain't got no deer." Seeing what I believed was a deer heart with fresh blood on it, and seeing fresh blood on the hunting knife was all I needed to do a legal search of the vehicle based on probable cause.

I asked the four men to exit the vehicle and then I searched the interior of the truck. I got a big surprise when I found an illegally killed doe on the floor in the back seat. The deer was covered with coats, clothes, and hunting gear. You see, the poachers did a pretty good job of hiding their deer by covering it up but they forgot one small detail, the heart on the console.

Poacher Bags a Tree

Most people respect the police. Most people would be willing to help an officer. Most people have positive contacts with law enforcement, police and conservation officers. It is crucial that officers of the law always remember to try to have positive contacts with the public even when ticketing or arresting them. Because of these positive interactions, the paybacks or returns from the public can be rewarding.

It works both ways. I appreciated all the times that citizens helped me or offered help over the years. I often think about these people and do my best to thank them and to show my respect back to them and everyone else that I come into contact with.

This willingness to help and assist the police was very apparent during this case where all of these guys from the bar ran out into the woods to offer aid to me. What a way to show their respect for the police. And so this story begins.

Another opening day of Michigan's firearm deer season was upon me as I patrolled all day and made several quality arrests. As always, I would take note of where hunters' vehicles were parked, the type, the color, and how long the vehicles had been parked in certain areas.

As the daylight waned and darkness fell, I saw several hunters walk to their vehicles, load their gear or deer, then begin traveling. Sometimes, hunters would take an extra hour or two to return to their vehicles due to tracking, gutting, or dragging deer, others from being a little lost.

Three hours after dark, I returned to check on a hunter's vehicle which I had seen earlier in the night. I pulled up to the hunter's vehicle just in time to see him closing his truck while he was still holding his shotgun. I walked toward the subject, and I could see blood on his hands and I politely asked him if he had had any luck. Without saying a word, the subject ran three steps and jumped into his already idling car. The now suspect ignored my order to stop, and in one quick motion threw his gun in the front seat, put the running car into gear and sped off. I yelled, "Stop! Police! Conservation officer, stop!" as the suspect accelerated and threw gravel on me.

I ran back to my patrol car, activated my lights and siren, and began the vehicle pursuit. The chase was on! All police officers know the adrenaline rush associated with a high-speed chase. In an odd way, police chases are really fun and exciting as we must outdrive, outthink, and outlast the bad guy. Unfortunately, there is also a bad feeling deep down inside an officer's gut coming from the fact that so many police chases end up badly. The want and need to catch a fleeing criminal is sometimes overshadowed by the thought of a sad and horrible outcome of a chase when an innocent civilian is harmed or killed. Many innocent families have lost loved ones as a result of police chases. The thought of injuring another motorist and the thought of being sued for engaging in a chase sometimes leads to the decision to terminate the chase and let the bad guy get away. Not this time, not me, not going to give up now, was the mode I was in.

I radioed St. Clair County Dispatch and advised them that I was in pursuit of a poaching suspect's vehicle and that the subject had a scoped gun in his front seat. I answered the usual questions, "road conditions dry, vehicle traffic light," as I chased the fleeing suspect. The chase was getting dangerous with speeds over 100 miles per hour now and I contacted dispatch. The radio traffic went like this: "The suspect is now speeding eastbound on M-136 approaching Wildcat Road, he is turning north (his left turn signal was on), no, he is turning right and going south, oh, wow, he hit a tree head on!"

To my amazement, the bleeding fool jumped out through his car window and began running. He ran behind a home and into a tall grassy field and toward a wooded area. He jumped out so fast that I did not even have time to shut off my siren. I hurriedly sprung from my patrol car and began chasing the subject. My vehicle pursuit now turned into a foot pursuit, one on one, and without the danger to other drivers. My kind of chase. Who's faster, who has more endurance, and who will win, the predator or prey? In the distance, I could hear the sirens from all sorts of emergency vehicles coming to my aid.

As I was running, I heard the unmistakable sound of something hitting a barbed wire fence. Ha, he was just ahead of me. I closed the distance to the suspect to what I knew was within tackling range, then proceeded to "abruptly" take him down. I placed the suspect in handcuffs and was holding him down when I noticed over twenty men walking toward me. It looked like something out of a movie, a large group of men walking toward me. The guys had all been in the corner bar, The Dorsey House Restaurant, and saw the whole thing and were coming to help me! The good citizens asked me if I needed any assistance. "No, but thanks," I said. What a honorable gesture to leave their cold beers and hot burgers to go afield to help a conservation officer. I thanked them and asked them to respond back to the intersection and wait to see if I needed any witnesses. I then proudly walked my handcuffed), bleeding, "catch of the day" suspect back to the accident scene. Several sheriff cars, firemen, ambulance workers, and bar patrons were waiting for me at the crash site.

I took the suspect to the EMT's who began first aid and eventually placed the suspect in an ambulance.

Inside the suspect's totaled car, I found his loaded 12 gauge shotgun in the front seat, and his illegally killed doe in his trunk. Timing is everything sometimes, and if I would have been delayed just a few seconds on my original stop of the suspect, the poacher would have escaped, he would not have wrecked his car, he would not have gotten arrested, and would not have had the trip to the hospital and then to jail.

This case involved a car chase and a foot chase. Each time an officer chases, runs down, tackles, fights with, or catches or arrests a suspect, the incident acts as a future deterrent to the suspect and for other people familiar with the case. In this particular case, let's add up all the people who got educated about poaching a deer. The suspect, the ambulance crew, all of the firemen and police officers present, the dispatchers, the guys from the bar, the onlookers, the hospital workers including nurses and doctors and all of the family, friends, and neighbors of all those mentioned above. It acts like free advertising to hopefully show other people not to break the law, or in this case, not to poach a deer.

Hunting or Working

Michigan Conservation Officers do not punch time clocks. For years, officers would work as many hours per day as they wanted. We were entrusted to work 80 hours during a two-week work period. However, working only 80 hours in two weeks was just not enough time to catch poachers, especially during peak activity periods. The months of October and November were extremely busy. Deer, fishing and small game seasons were all open in October and November, and the increased activity could keep officers working 24 hours a day. It would bother me to witness poaching or suspicious activity while I was not working, so I would work almost all of the time during these busy months. On many days, I would work 10 or 12 hours patrolling; then I would go hunting. On so many occasions, I would be enjoying my hunt but would be interrupted by poaching activity. So occasionally after working all day, I would take my patrol car when I would go hunting. I would hide it behind a barn or under a camo net or pine branches, then attempt to go hunting.

On one October afternoon, I sat in my tree stand in a misty warm fall rain. The damp, heavy air accentuated the autumn aroma of leaves, earth, and nature. Similar to how hunting dogs pick up scent easier on damp days, I relished the God-given smells of the outdoors. I was really enjoying the beautiful sights and smells of my bow hunt when I saw a very slow moving old pickup truck approaching on the gravel road nearby. The passenger window was down (in the rain, and then the truck came to a stop out in front of me and a scoped rifle pointed out the open window.

Bang. They shot right in front of me. Being archery season and seeing the scoped gun shoot from the truck, I knew I had the making of a good case. If only I could drive home, put my uniform on, load my patrol car, then drive back to the area, I might have a chance to catch the poachers. No, wait. My patrol car was only a half of a mile away! I ran and ran in hopes of getting to my vehicle while the suspects' truck was still close by. After sprinting the half mile through the woods, I jumped in and sped off, yeah. I was speeding, but I wanted to catch up to the truck. Soon I could see the tail lights of the truck which was still slowly road hunting. I activated my emergency lights as I pulled up behind the suspects, but then they accelerated. I sped up next to the driver's side door and with the lights flashing and sirens blaring, I looked face to face with the driver. Then he swerved at me as he tried to hit me!

Here I was, next to my poaching suspects in a police chase (only other police officers would know the feeling of adrenaline and excitement). I drew my handgun and pointed at the driver while still chasing the suspects. The driver saw the light (or my gun) and pulled over. In the front seat was a still loaded .22 caliber magnum rifle. I placed the suspects in handcuffs and began sorting everything out.

The passenger had sixteen warrants for his arrest; his bond totaled over $30,000 cash. I did locate the deer that they had shot. It was a small four-point buck, so I was able to charge them restitution for the deer. My deer hunt was successful. Times have changed, though. I'm not sure if taking a patrol car "hunting" would be allowed, but in doing so back then I was able to get the job done.

Gill Net Poachers Busted

Ever been fishing and the fish just aren't biting? Ever fished and fished for hours and could not catch a thing? It happens to all of us who fish. We change baits, use different colored lures and try different spots, but still can't catch a fish. Even though it is still relaxing and a privilege to enjoy the great outdoors and just enjoy the art of fishing, people still think it is nice to catch something. Some days, though, it seems like it is an impossible task even to land a fish or even to get a bite. On those days, no matter how hard we try, we catch no fish. But what if we could put out a ½ mile of fish killing gill net? Would we have a better chance of taking home some heart-healthy omega-3 filled fish? These guys thought so.

It was kind of fun but utterly disgusting, pulling up the gill net with my partner Jerry Prone and volunteer conservation officer Jim Purkiss. Huge salmon, trout, and monster walleye were already dead when we pulled the net into Jerry's patrol boat. I mean big, beautiful trophy fish, all caught in an illegal gill net. These were the fish that hook and line fishermen dream about. And if it weren't for us, the fish would have made it one hour away to some fish market.

It all started one night when Jerry got a complaint from a local fisherman. The fisherman said that he was fishing in Lake Huron near Lakeport State Park when his motor got tangled in some netting. When he tried to free his prop, he discovered the motor was hooked to hundreds of feet of gill net. Knowing that gill netting is illegal in the Lake Huron waters of Michigan, he became angry and called in a complaint. Jerry, Jim, and I responded to the area, and we observed an 18-foot aluminum boat on the lake without any lights, and two men in the boat were working the nets. We had to leapfrog along the shoreline so as not to lose sight of the fish poachers, but we also did not want to scare off the suspects. At one point, the boat with the two men in it began slowly coming into shore. We ran to the secluded beach to watch as the suspects pulled their boat into shore on the sandy beach. The two men were walking up along the beach carrying an ax and some firewood. We had called the sheriff department for backup, and Deputy Mike Bailey and Jerry, Jim, and I announced our presence to the suspects. They began to run immediately. Splashing along the water's edge, they ran towards their boat. We caught both of them. When I went to handcuff my guy, I realized that I was trying to handcuff a Paul Bunyan type dude. The big, burly nighttime fish poacher had such giant arms and wrists that my handcuffs would not even fit. After a little pushing and shoving, we put two pairs of cuffs on him and began trying to figure out who they were and how many fish they poached in our lake. Their boat had no lights, no registration, no life jackets and only gill net gear, axes, and firewood. They had stopped on the secluded beach to have a fire.

The sheriff department lodged the two men as Jerry, Jim, and I began pulling in the gill nets. These men boated one hour in the dark without any lights to set up their nets to steal our fish. All told, we ended up with 3000 feet of gill net, 700 pounds of game fish, and seized the poachers' boat and all gear and nets. The men were convicted by an impartial jury with a courtroom full of not so unbiased sports fishermen and women standing by. The local people who fished were infuriated by the poachers' act and were furious that they had killed so many of our trophy game fish. For years to come, I would get complaints from fishermen (who were not catching many fish) that the gill net poachers stole all the fish. Fortunately, our resources like fish, birds, and deer are a renewable resource, and the fish population did recover.

Lays Potato Chip Poacher

I watched a subject raise his bow and shoot a Canada goose right in front of him in the Black River. The hunter was using a compound bow with traditional deer hunting aluminum arrows tipped with three bladed razor heads. Most bow fisherman use bows equipped with a reel of line hooked to their arrow. Then they would use the line to retrieve fish, like carp and suckers, that they would shoot. This subject was just flinging arrows across the river in between the passing pleasure boats. Amazed at his good luck, I approached him from my patrol boat, and I checked his waterfall license. He then told me how he gets his geese after he shoots them. He said he uses a fishing rod and casts out and snags the dead birds and reels them in like a fish. Then I noticed that the hunter had an entire necklace made from migratory bird bands. Even the goose that he had just shot had a band on its leg. The bands are real trophies for waterfowl hunters, as each one tells a story. Each band has a particular serial number on it, and the United States Fish and Wildlife Service will respond to a hunter's request for information about where in the world the goose or duck came from. Some of the banded birds get harvested thousands of miles away from the location where they were banded. Anyway, the number of birds, the strange way the subject was hunting, and the number of bands he had collected piqued my interest. I talked to conservation officer Dave Shaw about the large collection of bands the bow hunter was collecting. Dave was one of our waterfowl experts in the state, and he agreed with me that something was suspicious, and we both believed that the hunter was only out collecting the coveted goose leg bands.

Two days later, the subject came back to the same location with his bow and fishing rod. I set up surveillance across the river. It soon became apparent to me how the subject could get such close shots at these banded geese. He opened up bag after bag after bag of Lays potato chips, and then sprinkled them along the shore. Then the hunter would just wait for the "city geese" to swim up for their snacks. He was very selective about which geese to shoot, only the birds with bands on them. The geese got used to being fed from people along the river. The subject figured out that he could bait the birds in close, just to collect more of the waterfowl bands. Then I ruined his fun, and arrested the subject for hunting waterfowl over a baited area.

Where Are All the Deer?

Public relations are a large part of a conservation officer's job. We are the front line for good and bad contacts with hunters, fishermen, and outdoor enthusiasts. Those who break the law and those who abide by the law, get on-the-spot attention while afield. Most contacts with hunters usually involve no illegal activity at all. However, many of an officer's contacts with hunters involve officers answering questions.

In recent years, one of the most common questions asked of conservation officers is, "Where are all the deer?" Typical answers include the following: The deer are hiding in the cornfields, hiding in the swamps, we had a harsh winter last year, it's too warm, it's too cold, it's too rainy, it's too windy, it's the wrong moon phase, there is not enough hunting pressure, there is too much hunting pressure, there are too many diseases, there are too many acorns, all of the deer have turned nocturnal, and there are too many predators.

While all of these reasons play a role in the number of deer sightings, their collective value does not outweigh the biggest reason for the lack of deer sightings in some areas. In certain areas, too many deer have been shot. Period. We need to save the conversation about deer management and population control for another time. But suffice it to say, that through

The author standing next to 53 hidden deer which all belonged to only three hunters.

liberal kill permits and an emphasis on reducing deer numbers, there are parcels of land where the number of deer have been drastically reduced.

So, asking, "Where are all the deer" is sometimes a legitimate question. Many hunters blame the DNR for issuing too many deer permits. Point well taken. But someone still has to use the abundant permits for deer numbers to fall.

Don't get me wrong. I realize we have a problem with wolf and coyote predation. I get disappointed when the weather is bad for hunting. Harsh winters and bovine diseases such as CWD and TB can have devastating effects on deer numbers, but I believe that the practice of "over killing" of deer in certain areas has the most negative impact. Many of the contributing factors for lack of deer are variables that are out of our control. But shooting too many deer in certain areas is something we control.

When asked the question about where are all the deer, I would usually respond by stating that, yes, I agree, the deer numbers are down. Then I would bite my lip to keep me from asking the question, "Have you checked your freezer?" Some of the same people asking about where all the deer are, were the same ones who killed six, eight, or ten deer the prior year. Hmmm.

An example of this is shown in an incident that I encountered only a few years ago. The incident involved three subjects that I stopped who had 56 deer that they had shot all hidden in their truck and trailer.

While working one night with my brother Mike in St. Clair County one November, we, along with St. Clair County deputies stopped a pickup truck pulling a trailer. The truck bed and trailer had cedar branches covering a lot of deer. Imagine our surprise when we walked up to the vehicle and located 56 deer hidden and all shot by just three occupants.

We counted, sorted, and counted and resorted the deer. All told, only three of the 56 deer were illegal. The other 53 deer were all legally tagged. The hunters kept telling us that there were too many deer and that the landowners had extra permits to use. I wondered if these same hunters wondered where all the deer were during the following years' hunts.

I also felt bad for all of the neighboring legal hunters in this particular area and other specific over-hunted areas when they see very few deer the following deer seasons. I suppose that they could legitimately ask, "Where are all the deer?"

Wet Seat

As I traveled to the Lapeer County Airport, I could feel the anticipation and excitement growing inside of me. I was looking forward to the flight that we were participating in later that evening. Several of our officers and the pilot met to lay out our plan to patrol for deer poachers by air.

After looking at county maps and figuring out who was going to work with who and which areas each ground unit would cover, we left the airport to head to our designated areas. We were going out hunting poachers, but on this night, we had some help. Our air support help was almost like cheating, as the spotter in the plane could see so much from the sky.

Once all of the officers were situated in their designated areas, we heard the booming radio traffic of, "Air one we are up." After about an hour of anxiously waiting, I heard, "Air one to 9-134." "Go ahead to 9-134," I said. The spotter in the plane was C.O. Ben Lasher and he advised me that they had spotted a subject in a wooded area shining flashlights all around. I responded to the area and I could see two subjects walking around in the woods, so I just sat blacked out for a while, to try to figure out what they were doing. After a while, I saw the subjects load two deer into their pickup truck.

When I drove up to the subjects with the deer, I contacted the hunters and asked them how their hunting was going. The driver told me that they had each shot one of the two small bucks that they had. Both bucks were tagged but the subjects' body language alerted me to check a little closer. Due to the vibes I was getting and also from the fact I had received poaching and baiting complaints in the exact area, I decided to try to verify their stories.

I asked the driver to show me where he shot his buck. He walked myself, Mark Papineau, and Sergeant Tom Wanless to an area in front of an elevated blind. He said that his deer fell in front of the blind when he shot it. But there was no blood, no hair, and no signs of a dead deer. The subject kept saying, "it should be right here," as he walked us around looking for blood. I climbed up the ladder and got into the subject's blind. I found no shell casings, but I did find something interesting, a hard plastic upright chair in the blind with over one inch of water on the seat. I asked the now suspect hunter if he was sure that he hunted in the elevated blind. He replied, "Yes, I killed my deer from that blind." I again asked, "Are you sure that this is the blind that you hunted in, and sure that that is the chair that you sat in?" He replied, "Yes, that is where I sat and shot my deer."

I climbed down and asked the hunter to turn around so I could see his backside. His hunting pants were dry, and he did not look like he had sat in water or had wet himself. I advised him that there was a slight problem with his story, and told him that his blind must have a bad roof leak. Bad enough that there was one inch of water on his chair. When I mentioned the subject's dry pants, he started rattling off confessions to me.

"You're right, I shot both the bucks tonight, and the six-point last night and..." I did ticket the subject for killing too many antlered bucks since the yearly limit is only two bucks per person. I also ticketed him for violating antler point restrictions.

Smashing Mailboxes

Sitting on my patrol car's warm hood on a cool October night was somehow a very memorable event. We would often shut our patrol cars off and get out and sit on a sleeping bag on our hoods so that we could listen for shots or see spotlights in the distance. It was something almost sacred. Only a conservation officer would appreciate the feeling of sitting on a warm hood of the truck, with our back resting against the windshield— all happening in the pitch dark on a quiet country road. Quiet, peaceful, and relaxing, all the while looking for poachers.

On one particular night, I was so comfortable and engrossed in the stars and outdoor sounds and smells that I hardly noticed the motor noise of an oncoming ORV. Then I heard WHACK, then another louder WHACK, and heard a fast approaching machine. I jumped off of my hood, then jumped into my car, and started it up. I turned on my lights just in time to avoid being hit by the three wheeler. The operator was driving without his lights on and never saw my vehicle parked on the road.

There were two males riding on the machine. They were traveling at a high rate of speed and were using a baseball bat to smash mailboxes as they sped along. I spun around and hit my lights and siren as the ORV sped away. The riders kept looking back at me while they were fleeing. I radioed St. Clair County Dispatch and advised them that I was engaged in a pursuit. After a couple of miles, the three wheeler tried to turn a corner too fast, and you guessed it, rolled over. I ran up to the upside down machine and tackled one of the riders as he tried to run. Then I noticed the second subject was trapped under the machine. I pulled the three wheeler off of the second subject. I then picked up their Louisville Slugger aluminum baseball bat and found all sorts of marks on it, some red, green, blue, and an assortment of colors from the multiple mailboxes that they had smashed. I towed their machine and arrested then for malicious destruction of property and fleeing and eluding police. How dare they interrupt my tranquil, relaxing patrol.

The Breadwinner

A nother time I had an interesting incident happened one winter's day right after we received two inches of fresh snow. St. Clair County Deputy Jim Stanley and I responded to an armed robbery call. Not just any armed robbery, or bank robbery, but an armed robbery at a day old bread store. Yeah, even though the store sells bread for 10 cents a loaf sometimes, a man with a handgun doing a holdup made us remember how serious the call really was.

We arrived on location and the apparently shook up clerk told us that the robber was wearing a blue jacket and was wearing tennis shoes. The clerk advised us that the man ran to the east across the parking lot. Deputy Stanley and I followed the tennis shoe tracks right from the bread store all the way to the door of a cheap motel nearby. Remember we had two inches of new snow, so it was easy to follow the running tennis shoe track. The motel was one of those budget, single story, flat roof, creepy joints that are featured in scary movies.

Anyway, we waited for more backup, and then we knocked and knocked on the motel room door. Eventually, a subject answered the door who said that he had been sleeping all day. Sure. We searched the cheap, dirty motel room and located $30.00 and a handgun used in the robbery. Nobody said criminals were smart. On the way to jail, we chuckled about the location that the subject chose to rob and the way that he forgot that he left footprints in the snow.

We also thought to ourselves that if the robber wanted to be the breadwinner in his family, then maybe he should get a job!

Yellow Curb Paint

W e all know what color yellow is used to paint curbs in parking lots. You know, that bright yellow concrete block looking thing that is placed at the back of a parking space to signal how far to pull into the space. Anyway, this story has something to do with that bright yellow paint.

One summer evening while I was patrolling the roads along the St. Clair River, I noticed a van ahead of me drive way over the centerline. The old hippy style van then pulled back into its proper lane and continued driving northbound. My concern for public safety made me follow the van to make sure that the driver of the van was not drunk or on drugs.

Following the van, I noticed the driver bend over and lean down between the front bucket seats. When he bent down, he swerved his van way across the centerline and into oncoming traffic. Luckily the van narrowly missed the approaching vehicles. Then the driver corrected his poor steering job and continued going north. Fearing possible danger to the other drivers, I decided to get closer to the van to try to find out why it was being driven so badly.

Was there mechanical problems? Probably not. Was the driver intoxicated? Probably yes. Was the driver distracted? Definitely yes.

As I followed the van, I saw the driver lean down between the front seats again, and the van swerved across the centerline again. I had seen enough and decided to stop the van to prevent a head-on collision.

I turned my flashers on, and the driver kept driving. After a bit, I hit my siren. The driver did a very slow head turn to look at his side view mirror. He then slowly brought the van to a stop. I walked up toward the old van and cautiously walked up to the driver's side window. Sitting there in the driver's seat was a very intoxicated, very stupefied man in his 50's. His body language and his slurred speech immediately signaled to me why he was driving so poorly. He was trashed! But there was something else unique with

143

the spaced out driver. He had bright yellow paint on his eyebrows, the tip of his nose, his mustache, his lips, and on his chin. I called for backup since I had no idea why this drunk guy had paint all over his face. Soon, Port Huron Police Officer Dave Seghi arrived on location, and we began our drunk driving investigation.

Along with the regular sobriety tests and questions, we asked the very intoxicated driver why he had paint on his face. He told us that he was sniffing paint to get high, then abruptly bent down between the bucket seats and showed us how! Oh my, he put his face into a five-gallon bucket of yellow paint and snorted a bunch of paint.

During our sobriety tests, the man randomly started explaining his sniffing paint routine. He discussed how he would drive around aimlessly and every so often would just lean over and snort and taste the paint. He said that the paint would get him stoned. Then he shocked us by methodically giving us details about which paint color worked the best. The subject told us that the bright yellow colored curb paint gets him the most buzzed.

Wow, that was really good advice coming from a man whose mind was half baked. From talking with the paint expert, I realized that he must have sniffed a lot of paint over the years. He was not the sharpest crayon in the box, but certainly one of the brightest colored.

Deer Decoy

Most everyone has seen video footage of unsuspecting hunters shooting at a deer decoy. Several wildlife shows on television show situations where officers set up decoys to catch road hunters or trespassers. Some people think that the use of deer decoys to be some sort of entrapment. The Michigan DNR goes as far as limiting the size of the antlers so as not to entice a semi-lawful hunter into shooting at a "trophy" stuffed deer. Umm, either a person would or would not shoot illegally at a deer from his car or on someone else's private property.

Using deer decoys does play a role in wildlife law enforcement. Although it does not take much talent just to put a decoy out and wait for a taker, many officers use very sophisticated mounted deer. Some decoy deer even move their antlers or turn their head by use of a remote control. The bottom line should be that no matter how big the rack is or how much the ears or head move, ruthless hunters should not illegally shoot at it.

I had set up a decoy along a gravel road in an area where there was a lot of road hunting going on. I hid my patrol car behind a barn, then climbed up into the hayloft to observe the setup. Soon, a slow rolling red pickup truck pulled up, and the driver glassed the buck with binoculars. Then the subject got out of his truck and shot at the fake buck. Then he walked 20 yards even closer and shot the buck again. Then the hunter crept to within 60 yards of the decoy and shot it again. He snuck up to about 40 yards from the deer and knelt down with his scoped shotgun, but before he could shoot again, I yelled out, "Stop shooting." You see, I did not want any more holes in the deer decoy. Immediately, the hunter yelled out hysterically laughing, "John you S.O.B., where are you?"

I got down from the barn and met the shooter near the deer. He said he saw the deer moving and knew that he hit it with each shot. My decoy was not a mechanical moving deer, but it did move a bit because the subject hit

145

the deer perfectly with each shot! I immediately recognized the subject as a trustworthy local man. Now I felt bad because a nice and dependable guy shot the decoy. Since the hunter got out of his vehicle before he shot, and since he used to have permission to hunt on the private property, I minimized the charges and just wrote him a ticket for hunting without orange clothing.

Thanksgiving Breaking and Entering

Law enforcement officers develop a "trained eye" that we use while on patrol to look for things that are out of place or that look suspicious. Being able to see things that others don't see is an admirable virtue to have as an officer. When we see something unusual or out of the ordinary is when our minds try to process that information and try to decipher if any crime has or is being committed. Seeing large rolls of wire with several dozen feet of wire hanging out of the trunk of a car driving past me caught my attention.

Thanksgiving morning arrived again, and I had only 8 hours of overtime for deer patrol. Back a few years ago, we went through a period when we worked as many hours as humanly possible—sometimes 20-30 hours straight in those days. But with budget cuts, came a reduction in payroll. Things changed over the years, so with only 8 hours to patrol, I knew I had to make my hours count.

We had about one inch of new snow in the early morning hours, so I figured the hunters (and myself) would have an easier time tracking our animals. Anyway, I was driving out near Emmett on a gravel road, when two shady looking characters in an old car passed by me. I looked at them but I saw no blood or deer and had no probable cause to pull them over. As the car passed by me, there was wire and cable sticking out of the partially closed trunk. They were dragging 50 feet of yellow wire behind them! Maybe they had serious wiring issues with their car or maybe not! I backtracked their vehicle tracks about one-half mile west to a building where the vehicle had been parked. I followed two sets of boot tracks to the building and I discovered a fresh breaking and entering! I looked inside and saw some partial rolls of copper wire. I ran back to my patrol truck and knew I had some catching up to do to try to stop the car with the wire dragging behind it. I sped up faster and faster as I headed eastbound.

Soon I could see the vehicle way ahead of me. After closing the gap, I hit the flashers, and then the car sped off. They then drove up a driveway and two males ran into a home. I ran after them but the door slammed ahead of me. I pounded on the door. I yelled and pounded and could hear voices and noise in the house. The car's trunk and backseat were totally full of rolls of copper wire. The trunk lid could not even close all the way, that's why the wires were sticking out.

I called for backup and then began watching the house to be sure the thieves did not get out. St. Clair County Sheriff deputies and Michigan State troopers soon arrived and we set up surveillance on the house. We tried everything to get the suspects to come out and to surrender. I knew they were inside, but no matter how many doors and windows we pounded on, we got no response. Our only option now was to get a search warrant. Being a holiday and all, it did take several hours for the paperwork. The problem was, I was almost out of hours by now, a strict 8-hour patrol is what I had, no more or less hours. So I had to lean on and count on my partners at the sheriff and state police to finish the job.

Some of my partners had to guard the home while the hours elapsed until a search warrant for the felons was delivered by another officer. In the meantime I had to leave and went home, showered, and went to our family's Thanksgiving celebration. Every hour, I would call for updates. Then, St. Clair County Sheriff Deputies Dale Mills, Lenny Coronado, and Gary Antilla started calling me, "Is your turkey good? How's the dressing, potatoes, and cranberry sauce? Don't worry, we are still out here, spending our Thanksgiving waiting." Another call, "How's the turkey, John? I felt bad in a way, but they were all my friends and we all knew that I would do the same for them. We have helped each other a ton of times.

Eventually, the sheriff deputies with search warrant in hand and with the only witness off at a holiday gathering, kicked in the door to the suspect's' home. They did find both felons hiding in the blue modular home. The handcuffed thieves told the deputies they thought no one would bust in to arrest them because of the Thanksgiving holiday. Wrong answer! Once we start a project, we finish it. If these criminals would not have been so greedy and overfilled the truck with wire, they would have gotten away with the break-in. They would also have been able to stay home to enjoy their own Thanksgiving dinner!

My phone rang again, "How's the warm apple pie, or is it pumpkin pie?" I laughed and apologized, thanked them, and had another piece of warm peach pie with vanilla ice cream on it.

Deer Rescued by Tow Truck Driver

Whitetail Deer. Most people love to hear about deer. Most people love to see deer, hunt deer, or talk about deer. Some people hate deer for reasons such as crop damage and car-deer accidents. However, when any of God's creatures are in peril, we all should have a kind heart and want to help out.

One such incident of a deer in need happened on a hot September afternoon. I received a call of a young male deer that had fallen into a six-foot deep basement window well. Don't ask me what the heck it was doing in there in the first place. So, I responded, and the poor thing was in the hot sun, panting, and was unable to climb out. I happen to really love deer, and besides as I said earlier, we all share in the obligation to help those who can't help themselves.

Deer hoofs are sharp and a wild animal's instincts would be to kick and fight off any contact with any humans, so we had a problem, even if we were just trying to help. I now had a dilemma. I could not leave the deer to suffer and die, nor did I want to get kicked about either. So I did the obvious? I called my friends at Preferred Towing. Maybe not so obvious, but I reasoned that if I could get a strap around the deer, the tow truck could lift him up to safety. Soon, the tow truck showed up, and my backup officer Deputy Tim O'Boyle and I guided him back to the deer. The tow truck operator, Jason Schultz, said he would be glad to help for free with only one condition, "as long as I don't have to go down there and hook it up," Jason stated. That's alright, that's what fearless cops with body armor are for I thought. So in I went, wrapped my little buddy up in a blanket, put a tow strap around the deer, and the tow truck lifted him up and out of the hole.

Dazed and confused, and cute, the deer just walked out of sight into a field and toward the woods where he belonged. Thanks, Jason and Preferred Towing. Jason was so helpful and was like many other tow truck drivers who are part of the first responder team. Jason was the type of guy that would help police officers in any way.

Jason heard that I was writing a book and thought it would be great if I wrote a story about the deer he helped rescue. Jason asked me when my book would be done. I told him, "Soon, later this year." A couple of weeks later in January 2016, while Jason was pulling a Jeep out of a ditch, some careless 18-year-old kid driver with marijuana in his system tried to pass Jason's tow truck on the shoulder and hit and killed Jason.

Along with the first responder team losing one of our own, Jason's wife and three young sons also suffered such a huge and devastating loss. The husband, father, little league coach, and all around great man died needlessly. We all need to be aware of the hazards of drunk driving, drugged driving, distracted driving, texting while driving, and careless driving to help prevent future tragedies like this one. Police, fire, medical, and tow truck operators all deserve the public's consideration, cooperation, and respect. I have been to many police funerals, several of those where the police officer was killed by errant, careless drivers. Please use caution and slow down when you see one of us along the side of the road while we are assisting and helping the community.

What Are You Looking For?

In police work and life, it is always good to be at the right place at the right time. Being in the right place and understanding the old adage that criminals always return to the scene of a crime, both played a role in this incident. Because returning to the scene of a crime is exactly what this person did in this story.

Another fall season patrol found me working with my VCO, Dave Houser. We happened to be northbound on a gravel road when I noticed a large shop-vac box with a deer hide sticking out of it. The box was lying in a shallow creek where it had been thrown off a bridge. I pulled over near the bridge, and we went down to the water to check out the box. We found the hide and legs from a skinned out deer along with some household garbage and some papers. One of the papers was a bank statement with a subject's name and address on it. What a lucky break, finding a name to investigate for the litter and the deer violation. Let's say the man's name on the paper was Joe Smith. Now Joe Smith was my subject.

Just then, a red Chevy pickup truck pulled up and stopped on the bridge and yelled down to us, "What are you looking for?" I walked up the bank to the subject's truck and saw an uncased shotgun in his front seat. I reached in and grabbed the subject's gun. It was loaded with three Winchester 12 gauge slugs. I advised the subject in the truck that he had a small problem and that he could not drive around with a loaded gun in his truck. I asked the subject for his driver's license, which he gave to me. When I looked at his license, I was shocked to read that his name was Joe Smith. There on the license that I was holding, was the same name and address that I had found in the box of litter and the deer carcass. I laughed and said, "You asked me if I was looking for something," and then I said, "Yes, you!" I explained the violation to the subject to which he then came unglued and confessed to all of the litter and deer violations. I thanked him for stopping and for asking questions and for offering help.

The Lookout Man was Busy Eating Pringles

The fall hunting seasons were finally upon us. As I drove around enjoying the October sights, I noticed a subject sitting on a guardrail along a very busy road. He was dressed in hunting clothes. Fortunately, I saw the subject before he saw me. I hid my patrol car and watched the subject to see what he was doing. The subject was looking all around, watching the road intently. His head seemed to be turning almost all the way around as he looked behind him, similar to how an owl's head turns around when it is hunting.

Anyway, the subject was nervous about something, so I continued to watch him. He seemed to be the lookout man for someone. Every so often, he would look down and get a potato chip from a Pringles can then look all around again. Each time he would be distracted with the chips, I got a little closer until I made contact with him. I guess the lookout man was so busy eating the chips that he never even saw me coming. The lookout man started to warn his friends, but it was too late. I spotted them dragging something in a blue plastic tarp. His friends had killed a deer illegally and were relying on their friend to warn them if the DNR came along. It was too bad for them, and a good thing for me, that their friend was too busy eating Pringles to alert them of my presence.

Hen Mallard and Eight Ducklings

Wild birds and animals really take care of their young. Somehow, the mother bird or animal knows to nurture and look after its babies. Parents feed, protect, groom, educate, and seem to love their offspring.

It is a sad but true fact that some wild birds and animals take better care of their babies than some humans do! Let me say that again, wild birds and animals sometimes make better parents than people do.

Just watch the news or read a newspaper to find out the disgusting way some people treat their children.

Anyway, one summer I watched a hen Mallard swimming along in the Black River. She had eight little, cute, fuzzy ducklings following her in a straight line everywhere she went.

The hen was always nervously looking around and especially looking toward the sky watching out for predators which may be after her young family.

As the summer progressed, I saw several duck and goose families around in my patrol areas. It is amazing how fast ducklings and goslings grow up. I kept track of the individual families by the number of ducklings the hen would have. I also used my spotting scope to determine how many young drakes and how many young hens were in each duck family. The color of the bird's beak is always the first identifying factor when sexing young ducks. Anyway, I figured out that this one particular hen had three young drakes and five young hens that followed her around.

During the summer, I watched this particular hen mallard with the eight ducklings several times, feeding, swimming, and playing in a specific area of the Black River. Then just a few months later in October, as I watched a salmon fisherman attempting to snag salmon with a fishing lure, the nine mallards which I had been watching, swam along the Black River in front of the fisherman. The salmon snagger cast three times at the ducks, and on the third cast, he intentionally snagged one of the ducks in the leg. The duck quacked and flew and struggled to get away as the snagger reeled and reeled and finally brought the struggling duck to shore. The fisherman then began stomping on the duck's head and while he was stomping, I ran at him and placed him under arrest. Oh, how tempting it is to do a little backwoods justice on some of these heartless, ignorant people. The duck was dead now, and not too surprising, the killer turned out to be a convicted felon. The other eight ducks flew away unharmed.

One week later, while I was working the same area, I observed two subjects hunting from a canoe while they trespassed on private property. The duck hunters saw the remaining eight ducks mentioned above and opened fire at the ducks as they swam in the Black River. The two hunters killed all eight ducks before they could fly away. Along with the trespassing violation, the poachers were also arrested for an over-limit of ducks. Six of the eight ducks killed were hens, at a time when the limit was only one hen apiece. It was a sad ending for one duck family.

Young Mallard duck killed by illegal fisherman.

Dangerous

A couple of years ago, I watched the owner of a tree cutting business climb to the top of a dead tree. The climber had a chainsaw, and I watched as he cut the top off of a dead Hemlock tree at a height of over 100 feet off the ground! The fellow climbed the dead tree with agility and grace and without any help from safety ropes or nets below him. The chainsawing man made several cuts and soon the dead tree lay in pieces on the ground. When the man was safely back on the ground, I walked up to him. He immediately recognized me and said, "Hi John."

We talked for a bit, and then he told me that he almost went into police work. He said that he wanted to be a conservation officer but that he just couldn't do my job because it was so dangerous. He said, "Yeah, you have the most hazardous job in the world, everyone you come in contact with has a gun. It's much too dangerous".

His comment struck me as funny coming from a guy who climbs dead trees with chainsaws.

Aiming At Deer With Scoped Muzzleloader From Van

The late muzzleloader deer season was almost over. It seemed as if all of the deer were dead from the never ending deer seasons of the year: youth hunt, early antlerless, veterans, handicapped, archery and regular firearms seasons. They had taken a toll on deer numbers over the three-month deer hunting marathon. After not seeing many live deer left, I was surprised and pleased to locate five deer feeding in a harvested sugar beet field. The deer were only 100 yards away from the road, and one of the deer sported a decent six-point rack on his head. I decided to keep an eye on the deer to make sure that no road hunters would come by and shoot the deer. After all, the six-point would make quite a trophy the next year if he could survive a few more days

Anyway, I hid my patrol truck and waited and watched for any illegal road hunters. Then, I saw a very slow moving white van turn down the gravel road toward the deer. The van had its windows rolled down and was going very slow. I knew the occupants were looking for deer. I began following the van, and the driver kept hitting his brakes (another sign of road hunting). Then the van stopped right out in front of where the deer were eating in the harvested field.

I was getting closer and closer to the now stopped van, when all of a sudden a scoped muzzleloading rifle popped out from the open driver's side window. I pulled up right behind the van, and the gun remained aiming at the deer. "Shoot," I mumbled to myself so that I could catch them in the act. "No, don't shoot the last buck," I thought. I turned on my flashers, but the gun remained shouldered by the driver, still pointing at the deer. The men in the van were so engrossed in what they were doing that they never saw my patrol truck or me walking up to their van. When I got up to the window, I easily saw the driver aiming at the deer through his muzzleloader scope.

The passenger said, "I bet John Borkovich is watching us right now." "He is watching you right now. Don't shoot" I stated.

Surprised (kind of), the men in the van said, we're not shooting deer, we are only looking at them with our rifle scopes. I then recognized both of the van's occupants. They were great guys, and I began to believe their story.

We talked and laughed at how guilty the hunters looked by aiming a gun out of their vehicle's window. I checked the gun and it was totally unloaded. No powder, no primer at all. I then checked the two guys and their van and found no powder, bullets, or primers. All they had was a scoped muzzleloader but nothing to make it shoot. The subjects explained to me that the driver had asked his wife for a pair of binoculars for Christmas (in a few days), but for now, he was just using the scope on his gun to look for deer.

Two really good guys, not lying, not poaching, but I had a decision to make (albeit a very easy decision for me). Should I write them a ticket for the gun? No. Was it illegal to have an uncased gun in a motor vehicle? Yes.

Why do we have laws prohibiting uncased and loaded guns in motor vehicles?

1) For resource protection

2) and for public safety

So, I asked myself, did these fine guys pose a threat to the deer that they were looking at? No. The gun was unloaded. They had no powder, bullets, or primers in the van.

I asked myself if the two guys posed any safety threat to themselves by having an uncased gun in their van. No, the gun could not have gone off by accident or on purpose.

So why would I write tickets for the uncased gun or road hunting? I wouldn't; I didn't. All I did was laugh and visit with the hunters for a while, then wished them Merry Christmas and said that I hoped they got binoculars for Christmas.

Elk Antlers Lead to Illegal Machine Guns

No one day is like any other day in police work. Officers never know what awaits during his or her next shift. That is one of the attractions to police work. Phrases like "never a dull day" or "never boring" are used to describe a police officer's work day.

Officers need always to be alert and ready as their day goes from very slow to action packed. Many times, routine traffic stops, routine complaints, and routine violations are anything but routine. Officers should never get complacent and drop their guard by thinking that their work is just routine. Officers must be ready and prepared and aware of dangers and twists that may arise from an otherwise mundane or routine contact.

One of my routine or "regular" stops occurred when I got a call about someone who was driving around with a set of freshly killed elk antlers in the bed of his truck. The antler base still had some blood on it and there was no kill tag on the antlers. There could be many reasons why the antlers were untagged, including that the tag could have blown off or have been lost. But, the situation still merited checking it out.

So, just "routinely" checking the antlers was my goal. I would just contact the hunter and have him show me his license or explain where the elk antlers came from, and I would be on my way, or so I thought.

The word routine is used quite often in police work. A routine traffic stop. A routine hunter check. A routine patrol. The caller on this routine complaint provided me with the subject's license plate.

I called my dispatch and soon learned that the owner of the truck had an extensive criminal record, including several felony convictions. The routine elk complaint began to get interesting as I figured that the subject with the large antlers may have used a gun to kill the elk (in Michigan, a convicted felon cannot use or possess a firearm).

I made a plan to respond to the suspect's home to check the elk and also try to make a felon possessing firearms case. My neighboring officer, Kris Keil, was training an ambitious, newly hired officer named Mark Papeneau and I thought that they might enjoy assisting me at the residence. Good training exercise I reasoned. Soon, it became a very good training exercise. We drove by the suspect's address and could see a freshly killed set of untagged elk antlers. Sweet, we now had probable cause to inspect the antlers. I also called for Chesterfield Township Police to send a couple of backup cars due to the suspect's violent criminal record.

We tactically approached the suspect's home and as we neared the front door, I immediately realized that we were in a bad situation. From the front porch, ready to ring the doorbell, we could see a .50 caliber Barrett rifle mounted on a tripod, we could see several other weapons strewn all over the place, including an AR-15 rifle. All of these weapons were in the home of a violent convicted felon who had already spent jail time for concealed weapons, resisting police, and other serious felonies. The suspect, however, was not home which gave us time to plan our next move.

We left a few officers behind to guard the house in case the suspect returned. We then responded to Chesterfield Police Department and met with detectives and command officers.

The author with some of the illegal weapons confiscated from a dangerous felon.

We obtained aerial photos of the suspect's house and got a search warrant to search his home. As one of the plainclothes detectives put on his bulletproof vest, another officer said, "Don't bother with that vest, that .50 caliber will go right through that vest like a knife through butter." How comforting. Then we went to execute the warrant. As we were beginning to execute our search warrant, one of the perimeter police officers advised us that the suspect was heading toward his house in his truck and was refusing to stop for the officer. Come to papa, we excitedly thought as we saw the suspect's truck approaching us. We had a warm welcome home party for him, complete with our Springfield .308 rifles and all. We all placed the intoxicated suspect into custody without any issues or shots being fired. We were glad that he was not able to get into his home, because we soon learned that the .50 caliber and several other weapons were fully loaded and no telling what might have happened.

After searching the suspect's home, we seized over 25 weapons including fully automatic assault rifles and weapons with the serial numbers drilled out. We also found thousands of rounds of ammo and rolls of detonating fuse wire. The elk was illegally possessed, as it came from a quarantined elk ranch. Not too routine I thought, as we carried dozens of illegal weapons to our patrol units. I guess there is no such thing as routine in police work because one never knows what situation might develop from just standard information.

Father and Daughter Team up Against Poacher

What is poaching? No, I mean serious poaching. It is certain acts, like killing animals out of season, killing them at night, or killing way too many fish, birds, or animals. Most serious poachers know exactly what they are doing. Most serious poachers try very hard not to get caught. The poacher in this story did a real good job of getting rid of and hiding evidence. He thought of everything, except one small single item.

Early November is a magical time of year in Michigan. The rut is on and a lot of hunters are either archery hunting for deer or looking forward to the firearms deer season opener, November 15th. Many are anxiously planning and waiting for the big day. Most people wait. Some cheat and start early.

One year, I received a call about someone who shot a deer with a gun during archery season. I spoke with the callers, who happened to be a father out with his daughter. They were out bow hunting and heard a loud shot on their neighbor's property, then heard an ORV drive up and thought that they could see someone loading a deer on the machine. The only problem was that I was almost one hour away and it was now almost dark. I asked the father and daughter if they could stay out in the cold woods and listen and watch for clues until I arrived. "Heck yes, sure we will" was their response. Long after dark now, I pulled up to the woodlot where the complainants arranged to meet me. Two cold but very helpful figures emerged from the woods and advised me of what had happened. While they were sitting in the dark, they heard the ORV drive south toward an old farmhouse, and then they heard a truck speed away shortly afterward. I thanked them for helping. Then they showed me where they thought the poacher was when they had heard the gunshot. Sure enough, I found blood and deer hair, and a spent 12 gauge slug casing nearby. Then I found ORV tracks and I followed them about one-half of a mile to nothing. The ORV tracks just disappeared when they got near

161

the driveway of an old house. A sure sign that the poacher, deer, and ORV left in a vehicle. I knocked on the door of the cluttered and rundown old farmhouse. The proverbial "junk yard dog" growled, barked, and lunged at me as I stood just barely feet out of reach of the chained beast. After awhile, an uncooperative homeowner answered the door. More barking dogs from inside of the house made it difficult for me to even hear what the man was saying. I had a very tough time getting information from the homeowner. He was not cooperative at all. "No one was hunting here, I know nothing," was all he kept saying. Reaching sort of a dead end, I took a chance and said, "Oh ok, there's probably no poaching or problems, but what are your sons' names?" Reluctantly he gave me two names, as he was totally unaware of how I got him to spit out their names. I said thanks (for nothing) and drove down the road. I called dispatch and had them run the names of the sons. One son lived three hours away, and the other about one hour away.

I sped to an address in southern St. Clair County and knocked on the door of a home where one of the sons lived. A female answered the door. When I asked to speak to her husband, she told me that he was in the shower. I said that I would wait. Soon the husband emerged all clean and dressed. I looked at his hands for any blood, but he must have done a good job washing, not a bit of blood remained. We talked, him being very guarded and confident that he had shot no deer, had no deer, and he was sure that he had no deer blood on him. Sometimes, an officer starts second guessing himself at this point. I said, "Ok, can I have a look in your garage?" I was hoping to find an illegal deer. The suspect said sure and opened the automatic garage door. He was right; there was no deer.

I looked at his truck, and then it hit me. The truck was still dripping wet from a very recent car wash. "Mind if I look at your truck?" I asked. "No go ahead," he said. I checked the truck very closely and was about to give up and believe his whole story. Then I noticed one single deer hair caught in a crack in the bed liner of his truck. I said, "Oh, here is a deer hair," and then the suspect corrected me and told me that the hair was from his golden retriever. I then showed him how a deer hair is hollow for insulation in cold weather and how it will break when bent and that a dog hair will not.

A few more minutes of conversation led to the suspect confessing to me. He did poach an eight-point buck, pick it up with an ORV, then loaded the deer and the ORV into his truck and left his dad's property.

After I had left his dad's home, the dad called the 34-year-old son and told him that I was after him. So the poacher drove the buck to Lapeer County, threw it in a ditch, then drove to a car wash to wash out any evidence, then showered to wash away any blood on him. He went to extreme measures to get rid of the evidence, but thanks to the great father and daughter witnesses and some intense investigation and interview skills, I was able to crack the case. It was very rewarding to win this type of battle, but one wonders how many times the bad guys get away with crimes.

Jus Suckas

Immigrants are a significant part of American history. Many of our legal immigrants have worked very hard to get ahead in life. Many have had tremendous contributions to our country. It has always been amazing to watch many immigrants become assimilated and Americanized, and become such good members of society. Most immigrants learn how to abide by our laws and customs. Unfortunately, there are always a few who learn how to lie, break laws, or go poaching.

The men in this story were new to America, and they were still in the process of learning the language and the values and customs. One has to wonder if the phrase "once a criminal always a criminal" applies to some people. I wonder if these guys were poachers back in their former country, or did they just learn the tricks of the trade while becoming Americanized?

My partner Jerry Prone and I watched a large group of fisherman one late April morning. The subjects caught quite a few suckers and then would put them on stringers in front of them in the river. Then one subject caught a pike and immediately stuck a stick all the way through the fish from the butt then out through its mouth. With the fish intact and with the guts still inside, he began cooking it over a campfire. Pike season was not open yet, and soon the suspects ate the pike, and disposed of the evidence. Then one of the subjects caught a largemouth bass. To our amazement, he then cut a hole in a two-liter Mountain Dew bottle, filled the bottle with water, and then put the bass in the bottle and hid the bottle in some weeds. Bass season was not yet open either, and now the illegal fish was concealed in a pop bottle that just looked like litter in the woods.

Jerry and I approached the subjects and politely asked, "Are you catching any fish?". "Jus suckas," is what they replied. "Oh, what kind of fish did you catch?" I asked. "Jus suckers," as the subjects pointed to the suckers on the stringers in front of them. "Are you sure you only caught suckers?" we asked. "Yes, jus suckas."

We walked to the bottle with the bass in it, and retrieved part of the pike carcass and then issued the suspects tickets for taking the bass and pike out of season. Again, if the suspects would have had the bass and pike on the same stringer as the suckers, we probably would have treated them differently. But when someone is deceitful enough to hide an illegal fish and eat the other the illegal fish, then I don't feel bad at all about taking law enforcement action.

Local Farmer Has Car-Deer Accident

To most of us, the sight of a deer is a beautiful thing. We love to hunt deer, scout deer, watch deer, photograph deer, and we are absolutely consumed by deer. Many of us have this affliction; Some people, however, really despise deer and wish that deer would become extinct. Due to the conflicts that deer pose with farmers, car insurance companies, and with the land's carrying capacity, some people just do not like deer.

One such deer hater is a farmer friend of mine. He is a family man, works hard, and pays his taxes. Just because he loathes deer doesn't make him an evil man. Most of the farmers understand the relationship between farming and deer hunting. Many allow hunters to enjoy the sport of hunting on their land. There are farmers, however, like this one friend of mine, who always complain about deer numbers even when the numbers are down.

One night, I responded to a call. A vehicle collided with a deer and the driver needed an ambulance. I reached the scene of the accident and immediately recognized the person involved in the car-deer accident. Of all people, the person who hates deer the most was the poor guy injured in the collision. I recognized his large farm truck and saw the farmer standing on the side of the road with his face all covered with blood. He had pieces of glass still stuck in his face and his eyes. Even though he was bleeding and his truck windshield was smashed out, he still had the wherewithal to tell me, "Look what your stupid deer did now, John."

The accident began when a six-point buck ran out in front of a female driving a minivan. When she hit the deer, it flew up and smashed straight into the windshield of my farmer friend's truck. The entire deer was inside the cab of the truck. The deer was in a big heap of blood, hair, and guts. I gave my farmer friend medical attention while staring in disbelief at the amount of damage that the deer had made.

Soon, other emergency workers arrived on location. After the EMT's helped my bleeding friend they asked me to show them the inside of the truck. We opened the driver's door and both female EMT's started gagging at the gruesome sight. "There's the liver," "there's the stomach," "there's the intestines," were some of the comments made. I felt sorry for the farmer. Maybe he was right, there were too many deer, especially on that particular road on that particular night.

Another Car-Deer Accident

In late November 2010, I was requested by the St. Clair County Sheriff Department Dispatch Center to respond to a car-deer accident. The deer was still alive and needed to be put down.

As I pulled up to the all too familiar scene of a vehicle on the shoulder of the road with its four-way emergency flashers on, I could see a young deer in the ditch next to the road. I exited my patrol vehicle and advised the car's driver and his friend that they needed to stay back as I reached for my handgun to put the poor deer down. But the deer had other plans. The deer looked at me, stood up, and took a couple of steps. I got a clear look at the animal's body. I holstered my gun and began surveying the deer for injuries. From head to hoofs, I studied the deer and couldn't see any blood, broken bones, or trauma. I walked closer to the deer, now being only five feet away from it and I still could not see any obvious injuries. I even thought about the possible disease, but noticed that the deer had good muscle mass, and no rib bones, backbone or hip bones showing. The deer's eyes and nose were clear.

Officers derive no pleasure in killing an injured animal and we search for any reason not to kill the animal. Now I was finding many reasons not to shoot it.

The two teenage boys could not believe what they were seeing as I walked up and started petting the "button buck" who only minutes before was going to be shot. I calmly talked to the deer as I petted his neck as someone would pet a horse, dog, or cat. I could hear the teens behind me calling their girlfriends and explaining to them what was going on. As it turns out, I figured either the deer was temporarily stunned, or that someone must have picked up a fawn in the spring, illegally raised it, and then just let it go on the to side of the road and it possibly was "bumped" by a car, causing some stunning effect.

We took pictures and the deer wandered off. I asked the teen boys if they still believed in Santa Claus and they said, "We do now" as I radioed dispatch and advised that I did not have to shoot the deer and actually petted the deer before continuing my patrol.

Again, the thought crossed my mind of what a heavy burden or heavy responsibility that I have by virtue of what is strapped into my holster. I alone make the God-like judgment decisions to end life, and I accept the task with caution, care, and honor.

The author and a white-tail deer which only moments before was (almost) going to being shot.

Burning Squirrels

Opening day of small game season signified another exciting year of hunting in Michigan. I noticed two hunters walking around their car, so I walked up to them and asked how their hunting was going. I also asked if they got any squirrels to which they replied, "No." "Oh, okay," I said as I spotted blood on their hands and pant legs. I again asked the men if they had shot anything and they said "No" again. "Alright, let me just check your hunting licenses, and you will be on your way," I said. I checked their licenses and then asked them what was in their backpacks and game pouches. They replied "Nothing." So, I asked to check their backpacks, and when I opened them, I got a surprise. The backpacks were full of burned fur and flesh.

The subjects had shot over the limit of squirrels, but the surprising thing was that they burned the squirrels (everything from their guts to their heads was still intact) to a crisp. I had to sort through the dead carcasses to count how many squirrels over the limit they had.

If a person has ever smelled burned hair or flesh, they never forget the stench. Anyway, the subjects told me that burning the squirrels with hair and guts intact makes the meat taste good. Okay, I thought as I issued them tickets, but no matter how many times I washed my hands I could not get rid of the burning smell. Maybe, my partner, Jerry Prone was right. Smells like that get stuck way up in your nose, even in your nose hairs.

Auto Parts Litter Case

We have been so blessed with natural resources. I appreciate our resources and respect and cherish the beauty around us. Lakes, rivers, forests, streams, ponds and so many other outdoor attractions become part of our lives. Many of us work and live to be able to spend as much time as we can enjoying these gifts. However, there are those around us who choose to damage or destroy our precious resources.

Opening day of spring turkey season found me on patrol with my father, volunteer conservation officer Walt Borkovich. It was early on Saturday morning and the sun was just rising as we patrolled northern St. Clair County at about 7 o'clock a.m. We noticed a pickup truck traveling down a dead end road in the Port Huron State Game Area. What got our attention was the fact that the driver's window was down. The very slow moving truck kept stopping, as if the driver was road hunting. I zoomed up on the truck and activated my flashers and signaled for the driver to stop. As soon as I had stopped my patrol car, we approached the subject's vehicle, and hurriedly got to the driver in hopes of seeing his loaded gun on his lap. But there was no gun, no hunting clothes, and no sign of poaching. However, the bed of the truck was full of old rusty auto parts. The light bulb lit in our minds, the suspect was searching for a secluded spot to dump all of the litter.

I stated, "Oh, I thought you were poaching turkeys," and never mentioned the litter, nor did we even look back at the litter. I did say however, "Oh you're not a poacher, sorry but I don't have time to talk with you because I have to go all the way to Lapeer right now." I spun my tires on the gravel road and sped off out of sight. Then I drove into the woods and hid my patrol car and waited to see if the subject believed my sorry story about going all the way to Lapeer.

Soon the truck drove past us, and when he was almost out of sight, we began following the vehicle. After only three miles, the truck backed into a DNR parking lot. The subject must have thought that we were in route to Lapeer or something because as we watched with binoculars, he started carrying auto parts from his truck and began tossing the parts over a cliff toward the river. The cliff happened to be a very steep gravel bank along Mill Creek. The subject carried items such as transmission covers, oil pans, camshafts, and other large heavy pieces of metal. After the subject unloaded the entire truck, he got into his truck and began to drive away.

Oops, I guess we had not headed to Lapeer, because we immediately pulled the subject over as he exited the lot. The litterer had just began driving out onto the road when he saw us. We explained that we saw the whole thing and that the suspect was going to be ticketed. We explained that the auto parts would still be down by the river in 100 years and that would not be a good way to treat our environment. So we made a deal with the litterbug. If the subject walked all the way down the cliff and brought all of the litter back to his truck, then we would not take him to jail. We would just give him a ticket and send him on his way. SCCSD Ed Ogden did respond and stayed on site to witness the cleaning and restoration taking place.

So the strong, athletic, young litterer walked all the way down the hill and then carried a transmission cover all the way back up the very steep hill. Breathing heavy and sweating, the subject went back again and again. Each trip down the hill took over 20 minutes. We watched as an old fashioned justice system was unfolding right in front of us. On the subject's next trip, the litterer carried two camshafts and an oil pan all the way up the hill, and then (sweating and pale) asked us if it was all right if he threw up. I said, "Sure, go ahead and then finish your job." I almost felt sorry for him as he carried more litter then he heaved again. When he finally finished, I gave him the ticket. We laughed at the litterer for the throwing up part, but we also smiled due to the fact that we were able to catch him as he was thoughtlessly and carelessly ruining our land.

Be Back in Fifteen Minutes

My brother-in-law and my wife's sister were over for Sunday dinner one day in March 1990. Being an FBI agent, my brother-in-law was interested in my job, so I offered to take him for a quick ride in my patrol car. I told my wife that we would be back in a little while. Maybe 15 minutes or so, I said. As we headed out the door, my wife stated, "I have a warm Sunday dinner, so please don't be gone long." So we went for a short ride along the Lake Huron shoreline.

Suddenly, a dirt bike dangerously darted out in front of us. The motorcycle was weaving between the cars on the very busy road, so I decided to stop him. I hit the flashers and signaled for him to stop. The subject on the cycle looked back at me and accelerated away. It was on. With sirens blaring and lights flashing, we sped up toward the cycle. Once again, I was in a chase; the adrenaline rush hit us. The chase temporarily ended when the cycle drove off the road and through a large group of pine trees. We drove as far as we could and then got out and began tracking the motorcycle tracks on foot.

Knowing that dinner and wives were waiting, we made the logical decision just to give up the chase and go home. No, we didn't! We wanted to catch the fleeing subject. We did not have cell phones in 1990, and we had no way to call our wives to tell them of the delay. We tracked for about an hour and then found the motorcycle buried in a brush pile. Running the VIN number on the cycle yielded the fact that the owner was a convicted felon on parole.

Now we could not give up on the chase even though the dinner would be cold and the wives would be even colder. Well, after three hours, we did track the subject down, and we eventually made it home to our not so happy wives. "I thought you were going for a 15-minute ride," was all we heard. Sometimes a real man has to do what a real man has to do. Besides, there are lots of good restaurants out there anyway.

Felons Hiding Out in State Game Area Cabin

In a way, I understand and appreciate the concept of "preppers" living off of the land and being prepared for doomsday. I have seen books and magazines which illustrate ways to be self-sufficient by hunting, fishing, gardening, and other methods of survival. Being prepared for power outages, terrorist attacks, and any other emergency is something we should all strive for.

Being a survivor, and being prepared to survive is actually a good thing. Myself, and a lot of other people I know, will not be the ones waiting on a rooftop with a sign begging for someone else or the government to save us. I will save myself. The save yourself, fend for yourself, and be prepared for anything attitude is a good way to live. Especially for law-abiding citizens...

But when criminals hide out and isolate themselves in remote areas, it's different. The following story of a criminal hiding out in the woods took place in the Port Huron State Game Area.

The Port Huron State Game Area includes land situated along the Black River in St. Clair County. Steep cliffs and a dense coniferous forest along the river makes one think that they are up north, out west, or in Alaska or somewhere really wild. Because of this rugged area, I was surprised when I received a call that a hiker had found a makeshift cabin hidden in the Pines, Cedars, and Hemlocks way out in the woods. I walked and searched and walked and searched and finally found the cabin. Unsure of why someone would hide a cabin so well, I decided to carefully check the area. I found survival manuals, canned goods, vegetable and fruit seed packs, and clothing and ammo. Someone was planning to stay in the woods for a long time. Why would someone try so hard to " live off the grid" by planting gardens and living off the land here, I thought. The cabin was so well hidden, and it was also covered with Pine and Cedar boughs, which made it impossible to spot from an airplane or helicopter. The spot chosen was so thick and had such a dense canopy that it could not be seen from the air anyway. Being suspect of the cabin and its belongings, I followed a very lightly used trail for about one and a half miles to an old pickup truck oddly parked. Upon checking with dispatch, the registered owner of the truck came back as a convicted and wanted felon. I began watching the truck and found out that every three or four days, someone would leave a newspaper and food items in the truck. Then one day, a white car with Colorado plates was parked next to the pickup truck. Upon checking the owner's status, I found that he was also a convicted felon who was also wanted in Michigan and Colorado. There was an empty gun case and .22 LR ammo inside the Colorado felon's vehicle. Great, I thought- now there are two armed felons holed up in a cabin hidden in the woods.

I asked the sheriff department for back up so I could walk up to try to arrest the suspects but (understandingly) was told no, that situation was too dangerous. Then I called the state police and was told that we should not approach the cabin due to the suspects' advantage over us. I contacted the SWAT and E.S. teams around the area and again was advised that the cabin's approach would be too dangerous. The DNR supervision advised me not to attempt to arrest the suspect at the cabin because of the danger involved.

There I was, in a quandary, no one wanted to risk officers' safety but I could not just leave these dangerous felons living on our state land. What if some unsuspecting hunter or fisherman or hiker was harmed by these criminals? I owed it to the public to keep them safe. After a few days the white car left, so I went in to get the remaining felon. By myself, I carefully snuck up to the cabin, found fresh signs of activity and methodically surveyed the very dangerous area. Then I noticed an unkept subject with a long black beard wandering around in the woods. I followed him for hours until he made a turn and headed toward his truck. I ran to my patrol vehicle and set up a distance away and waited for the suspect. I called for backup when the felon entered his vehicle. To my surprise, he began driving the truck. I followed him for a distance until I could see the two waiting St. Clair County Sheriff Department patrol cars ahead. Then I sped up and we conducted a felony stop on the unkept felon. The wanted man surrendered without a fight, and I was relieved to rid the woods of the potential hazard.

After spending the next year in jail, I found out that the felon had traveled to Nevada where he was shot and killed execution style while he was possibly involved in drug activity.

Follow the Breadcrumbs Home

T he grass is always greener on the other side of the fence. This common metaphor sometimes resonates with hunters. Some misguided people think that all the deer are on the neighbor's property. Since hunters spend a lot of time alone in the woods with nothing to do, their minds often wander. Some of these people talk themselves into thinking that the deer hunting is better anywhere else but where they are hunting. The next step in the delusion is to believe that it's not fair somehow that someone else could have better deer hunting than they do. This puts the hunter into an "I'm going across the property line and onto someone else's land to hunt" attitude.

We have a major trespass issue. Trespassing is an age old problem that causes many other problems. Many states have tried to address the trespass issue. For example, in Florida, trespassing is a felony and in Texas, trespassing in taken very seriously. Trespassing poachers in Africa can even be shot and killed. Trespassing seems like a minor violation to some, but in reality, trespassing is a serious intrusion into someone else's land, privacy, and security. Many other issues arise from the act of trespassing. Some trespassing leads to crime ranging from poaching, cabin break-ins, cattle rustling, and tree stand thefts. Remember the out of sight, out of mind principle. Yes, if someone was not trespassing in the first place, they would not have seen the cozy cabin in the woods or an expensive ladder stand. I believe that I was one of the toughest conservation officers Michigan ever had when it came to trespassing cases, and I made a lot of them!

One of my trespassing cases occurred on an October day while I was patrolling for deer hunting activity. I noticed a teal green car parked along the road near the State Game area property. There was no violation, the vehicle had no suspicious signs but I still made a mental note of the license plate and kept working. What made the car stand out to me was that the vehicle had been parked in the same spot for the entire day, from long before light in the morning until long after dark.

The following day while checking some private property adjacent to the Port Huron State Game area, I found some drag marks and then found a little blood along the drag marks. The drag marks were heading away from the private land and going toward the state game area.

Checking for evidence around the area, I found a second blood trail that met up with the first drag marks. I backtracked the one drag mark to a gut pile, then I backtracked the second drag mark and found another gut pile about a half mile away to the east. I gathered lots of evidence including deer hair and deer blood, and boot track identification, but the real telltale clues of this case ended up being small pieces of orange plastic. The small pieces of orange plastic belonged to some tarp that the deer were being dragged on. You see, every once in awhile, a piece of the orange plastic would rip off when it got caught on a branch or a sharp stick, and it would leave a piece of evidence behind. I followed the orange pieces of plastic through the private land and under a fence, then the trail led across the state land and ended up at the spot where the teal green car was parked the previous day. Now I had to connect the dots. I ran the license plate that I had seen the night before through St. Clair County dispatch and found out that the vehicle belonged to a subject who lived about six miles away. I spent the remainder of the day searching for the suspect, then at about 9:00 p.m., I located the vehicle at the suspect's residence.

"No, no deer. No, no trespassing. No, no violations, no violating" "No, no, no, no," was all I heard the suspect say as I asked him questions about the day before and his deer hunting experience. After about 20 minutes of interviewing and several "no" answers, I calmly said to the suspect, "Okay, I believe you, but before I go, could I get a quick look at the trunk of your vehicle?" "Sure, I have no deer in my trunk," said the suspect. He walked me out to his car, and he was right, there were no deer in his trunk, but there was something else that I was interested in, an orange plastic tarp with deer hair and blood on it. Amazingly, the tarp had several small missing pieces. I took several small pieces of orange plastic from my evidence envelope, and then I asked, "Do these look familiar?" Like Cinderella's glass slipper, the orange pieces fit. "Yeah, you got me," and without any confrontation, the suspect showed me a six-point buck and a button buck that he had killed on the private property. He then explained how he dragged the deer on an orange plastic tarp all the way up to his vehicle. The suspect gave me a written confession of how he trespassed on the private land, and then

176

dragged the deer out under the cover of darkness. The orange plastic tarp had two important functions. It helped him drag his deer more easily, and the tarp ended up helping me as well by leaving some very important clues behind. The small pieces of plastic helped me solve yet another trespassing case.

Two Spotted Fawns Poached

Poaching, car accidents, farming accidents, wolf and coyote predation, and other types of mishaps sometimes leave fawns as orphans. I brought home several newborn orphaned fawns during my career. My family and I bottle fed and raised a few of the fawns. We would rehabilitate them, and when they were healthy enough, we would release them back into the wild. Fawns are the definition of cute. They are simply adorable little creatures. They are so sweet, gentle, lovable, and innocent. When I would care for the little orphans, I would become attached, and I loved the little buddies. Sometimes, while looking at the fawns, I would wonder how I could enjoy hunting deer so much. But I love to hunt mature deer that have learned how to hide, run, sense danger, and sometimes even turn nocturnal to help assure their safety. I get no enjoyment from hunting very young deer, and I would never even think about killing a spotted, defenseless, and innocent fawn. Some people would though.

One year, my great partner, Jerry Prone, received a call on opening day of small game season, September 15th. It was a beautiful September day that greeted the small game hunters all around the state. The caller told Jerry that he saw three deer walk past him, then heard two shots right where the deer went, and only saw one deer come back his way. The small game hunter said that only the adult doe came back out from the woods, and that the two small fawns were not to be seen.

Jerry and I went for a walk to check for any evidence of a possible poaching situation. We searched and searched, and then we found drag marks, deer hair, and deer blood. We then found where two small deer were gutted. Whoever killed the deer actually attempted to hide the gut piles with large dead logs and brush. We followed drag marks, hair and blood all the way to the backyard of a subject that we were already familiar with. We drove up near the suspect's driveway and found a white garbage bag set out with the household garbage. We looked in the bag and found the hides and legs of two very small spotted fawns. The hides both had bullet holes in them. Then, Jerry had a great idea. He said since the subject had a small herd of captive deer in his fenced yard (under DNR permit), he thought that we could walk right up to the subject's door and ask him if a couple of his fawns escaped. Then we would ask him if he had to put the deer down. Great idea. We asked the subject straight out, "Did a couple of your deer escape?"

The subject said, "Yes, two fawns got out, and I had to shoot them." Just like clockwork, he fell for the trick. We knew the deer he shot were from the wild and not deer from the pen in his yard. After speaking with the suspect for awhile, he admitted to poaching the two spotted wild fawns. We then had the suspect write out a written statement about killing the two fawns (a full two months before firearm deer season). The subject did confess and gave us the meat from the two deer. All of the meat from the two deer fit into a very small white kitchen garbage bag. Less than ten pounds of meat was all there was from the young deer. That was ten pounds total. The fawns were born late and were still in their summer spotted fawn clothing. They looked like they each had a live weight of about twenty-five pounds. It's pathetic to poach and even more pathetic to poach such small, immature, and innocent young animals for ten pounds of meat! We arrested the subject, and 72nd District Court Judge Cooley sent the poacher straight to jail for weeks. The term started right then on December 23rd. The defendant pleaded, "But I don't have a toothbrush, and what about Christmas?" Judge Cooley, who was disgusted and angry at the fawn poacher, said, "I don't care if you miss Christmas, and I don't care about your toothbrush. Now go directly to jail you poacher!" Consequently, the DNR then revoked the poacher's license to own and raise deer.

Grabbed Something in Bed of a Truck

Police departments all over the world have a multitude of policies and procedures pertaining to the use of deadly force. Court cases have stipulated reasons why an officer can use deadly force or the threat of it. However, there is no law or policy which signals or directs an officer's mind to draw his/her weapon. Sure, policy permits the use or displaying of a firearm to save a life or to protect an officer's life. But, each critical incident is different. There is no way to direct when it would be permissible for an officer to draw his/her weapon for every occasion. Only an officer knows when it's time to use a weapon. There should be no hesitation on an officer's part about when it is appropriate to draw a weapon. Some instances need no thought. One such automatic situation occurred one night in Port Huron.

On this particular stop, when I felt the knee, I broke leather. Breaking leather is a police term, sort of vernacular for when an officer draws his/her gun from their leather holster.

Trust me, when I saw all of the people in the truck moving around and then when I felt the human knee (dead or alive) buried under garbage and sleeping bags, I needed no prompting or policy allowing me to draw my gun. The "It's game time" feeling came over me, and I drew my .40 caliber Sig Sauer.

This situation all began one late night in July while I was checking walleye fishermen. I was in route to the St. Clair River in downtown Port Huron when I noticed a pickup truck driving very fast and recklessly. I turned my flashers on and signaled for the driver to pull over. The truck did stop and I noticed six or seven people in the cab of the truck who were moving all around as I approached the vehicle. These movements are called furtive gestures and are usually associated with subjects hiding contraband and weapons. A bad feeling came over me as I cautiously walked up toward the driver's window. I stopped along the bed of the truck to try to see what all the commotion was about inside of the truck. I then glanced down into the bed of the truck and noticed that it was a jumbled up mess of sleeping bags, blankets, sacks, and garbage bags. Police intuition kicked in. I reached down and grabbed one of the blankets and got a big surprise. How or why this happened I don't know. Why I picked that exact spot to feel, I still don't know. But when I grabbed the old blanket, I was holding onto a knee-somebody's knee. The distinct feeling of a knee cap put me into battle mode since I had no idea if the covered and buried knee belonged to a criminal or if it belonged to a dead person. Reach down and grab your own knee right now. There is no mistaking of what a knee feels like.

Gun drawn now, I commanded for everybody to hold still, and I called for backup. As backup arrived, we lifted up the blankets and garbage bags to find two guys hiding who were scared and a little tired from their ride all the way from Detroit. I then had the nine subjects exit the vehicle and was able to determine that some of the travelers were illegal aliens. I was glad that the travelers were alive and well, at the same time I was happy that they did not have any guns or weapons on them. Shocked I was, that the one place I put my hand, happened to be on a person's knee. Some of the things that we see are so crazy and odd. You just can't make this stuff up. These incidents just seem to happen while on patrol.

10-point Buck Poached During Bow Season

S hooting a 10-point buck seems to be the pinnacle of deer hunting. For me, from a young age, hearing about a 10 point buck has always signaled a trophy. Most hunters dream about them. Sure, seeing and possibly shooting any buck indicates a trophy to many hunters, as all deer are trophies in their own way. Boone and Crockett scores have great significance to many hunters. Also, there are some great eight point buck trophies. But, all in all, it's the 10-point buck that denotes a big buck. Most hunters never do get to harvest a 10-pointer. Some need to cheat to do so.

This story is about a big 10-point buck that never did get to become a cherished trophy to a licensed hunter. The events of this story took place during the quiet period in Michigan, which is just before the firearm deer season. This quiet period limits hunters to archery gear, shotguns with birdshot, and .22 LR weapons. No centerfire rifles or shotguns with slugs or buckshot can be in possession while afield.

It was November 10th, the rut was on, and archery hunters were hunting hard and enjoying this exciting period just before the firearm season. One landowner was enjoying the quiet outdoors when he heard a gunshot on his land in the late afternoon.

A short time later, the landowner went to where he heard the shot, but he was too late. The only hunter who had permission to hunt on his land was gone. The landowner found a fresh gut pile only 25 yards away from one of his blinds, and he found a spent 12 gauge, 00 buckshot shell casing in his blind. After speaking with the landowner, I asked newly hired Michigan Conservation Officer, Ken Kovach, if he wanted to work with me on a case for a little training and a lot of fun.

We responded and collected evidence and took photos of the area. The 12 gauge shell was real fresh. It had that memorable smell of a newly fired shell casing. The gut pile was fresh and we were confident that the deer was killed by a poacher with a shotgun and not by an archery hunter.

The landowner supplied us with the name of the hunter who was using his blind and we began our frantic search for him and the deer. But time was of the essence, the longer it took to find the deer, the less of a chance we had to get the evidence we needed. We checked several residences and followed up on possible locations of our suspect. No luck, and just like the television show "First 48", we were losing valuable time. We finally got a cell phone number for the suspect. After six or seven hours we were finally going to get a chance to speak with the possible poacher. I called the suspect and he abruptly told me that he was hunting up by Port Huron and that he did shoot a big 10-point buck with his bow. I had already checked the suspect's record and found out that he was a convicted felon. Being a felon prohibited him from owning or possessing a firearm (or go hunting with one). The suspect was very convincing about his "bow" kill. During his description of his successful hunt, I asked him several questions that had no meaning and no importance to the case. The suspect answered all the questions, even the one trick question.

See, all the questions were dummy questions except for one. Was it a big buck? "Yes." Did you make a good shot? " Oh, yes." Did it fall right down? "Sure did." All bait questions. Then I asked him in quick fashion, "Oh, where is your buck now?" Without thinking, the suspect said, "At the deer processor in St. Clair Shores." A few more dumb questions followed, then I congratulated the subject and hung up. The panic was on! We had to get to the processor before the suspect did.

Now being eleven o'clock at night, we sped over to one of the well-known deer processors, but the shop was closed. We contacted the owner at his home next door. We asked to see the deer that the hunter had brought in. The owner opened up his shop, and we noticed a caped out ten point buck right up front and checked the tag on it. Indeed, it belonged to the suspect. We asked the deer processor about the buck and asked him if he noticed any bullet holes in the hide when he skinned the deer. "No, nothing like that, nothing out of the ordinary archery kill," he replied. Needing to check the deer and hide for gunshot bullet holes, we laid out the hide and head. We then checked the cooler where the skinned buck was hanging. Nine .30 cal. bullet holes were spaced out in the hide and carcass and punched through the hide just behind the shoulder. Oh, by the way, a 2-3/4 inch 12 gauge 00 buckshot round contains nine 30 cal. round pellets. What a coincidence. And the deer processor, what a liar to have not noticed nine bullet holes in a huge buck shot in archery season supposedly by a bow and arrow. We confiscated the

183

deer and wrote the processor a ticket for possessing an illegal deer. Yes, he should have called the DNR to report the gun killed deer being brought in during bow season, and yes he should not have lied to us about the deer.

I called the suspect and now being after midnight, met with him to lower the boom on him. We interviewed the suspect who admitted to killing the big buck with his 12 gauge shotgun using 2 ¾ inch 00 buckshot (surprise). This is true poaching. A convicted felon taking a shotgun into a hunting blind and then shooting a big ten point buck during bow season is definitely a poacher. He stole a buck from a legal hunter. He stole the coveted 10 pointer, which lives in many hunters' dreams. The poacher plead guilty to all counts, lost his hunting license for three years and lost his firearm, and paid thousands of dollars in fines, costs, and restitution. It took a lot of hard work and good investigative skills to make this case.

Unfortunately, a court slip up and a DNR computer slip up allowed the poacher to buy a hunting license the very next year. It is so frustrating to do my job only to have a technical computer glitch or administrative error put a damper on my good case. It took awhile, but the poacher finally got served the proper license revocation paperwork. Good riddance.

Quiet Period Case: Almost Too Many Laws

Hunters, fishermen, and officers sometimes believe there are too many laws pertaining to natural resource protection. One almost needs to be a county lawyer to interpret the hunting and fishing digests published by the DNR each year. Do this, and don't do that, this is illegal, that is illegal, this is prohibited, and similar verbiage is littered throughout the 62 page hunting guide for example. So many laws and so many rules sometimes create animosity between the DNR Conservation Officers and the public. It seems with so many laws everyone breaks the law sometime during their outdoor career. Minor violations such as not immediately tagging a deer upon killing it (how soon is immediately?) or someone taking their "hunter orange" hat off for a couple of minutes while adjusting their clothing, or a hunter not unloading his/her firearm after the exact end of legal shooting hours would all constitute game law violations and all would be misdemeanor arrests.

Many "violations" are committed without any ill intent or guilty knowledge. This needs to always be on an officer's mind when confronting outdoor enthusiasts. Warnings and education should be standard practice for most of these minor violations. With so many laws on the books, it seems difficult to ascertain which ones are serious and which ones are not. To an experienced or understanding officer, there is not much doubt upon the severity of a violation. The circumstances matter!

Take a quiet period violation for instance. "Quiet period laws" in Michigan stipulate that a person cannot possess (afield) a centerfire rifle, or a shotgun with slugs or buckshot during the November 10th thru the 14th period just prior to the firearm deer season opener. This seems overprotective to some. Again, how and when this law is applied is the key to resource protection and good public relations.

An example of the use of this law happened a few years ago on November 13th in northern St. Clair County. One evening while I was patrolling, I located a pickup truck parked along a road near a large wood lot. Yes, the small game season was open, but upon looking into the cab of the truck, I noticed an empty gun case and a box of Remington slugs.

I quietly walked through the woods, and after awhile, I saw the outline of a subject in full camo sitting at the base of a giant white oak tree. At 40 yards, the subject saw me and ejected five shells out of his Mossberg model 500 pump shotgun. I approached the subject and then reached down and picked up five Remington 12 gauge shotgun slugs from the atop of the leaves near his feet.

We had a nice conversation and then the subject admitted to me that he was starting two days early with slugs because there was a 14 point buck living in the area and he wanted to shoot it before his neighbors did on opening morning.

Some laws seem minor, but to me and his neighbors, the circumstances of this law violation was anything but minor. Stealing a trophy buck while dressed in camo and hunting with a shotgun and slugs two days before firearm season makes one of the "minor" laws seem more like a major violation!

Baby Geese Killed by Gunman

Goose populations have grown in numbers so much in some areas that their high numbers have caused a conflict with humans. We all know what the conflict is. It's not the sight or sound of the geese that offends people. It's not that the geese are eating too much vegetation or anything. It's the "landmines" or in common terms, the poop piles they leave behind on people's docks, boats, lawns, and property that cause problems. The abundance of these messy, smelly excrement piles is so offensive that wildlife agencies have changed the season opening dates and have liberalized bag limits in an attempt to trim the goose numbers. As the population of geese has exploded in particular areas, the conflict with humans has also increased. Hunters want more animals and birds to hunt, but there is a point where the populations grow so fast that the bird or animal creates a public nuisance. Geese have adapted and often become "city geese" and over populate in spite of liberal bag limits and extended seasons. DNR and U.S. Fish and Wildlife agents have even resorted to netting and trapping young geese to relocate them by the thousands. Wildlife officers have even been involved in "egg shaking" to control goose numbers. In some areas, nothing seems to be working, and the goose population is so high that the left behind fecal piles become a contentious issue. One homeowner decided to handle the problem himself.

One day, on a warm June afternoon, a boater called to report a man shooting at geese with a shotgun and stated that there were goose feathers everywhere. I needed to get to the small island where the man was shooting in a hurry but had no time to jump into my boat and motor there. So I called the St. Clair County Sheriff Department, and luckily they had a patrol boat in the area. I jumped into their boat, and we motored up to the suspect's seawall. The homeowner ran into his house carrying a shotgun when he saw us. We jumped out of the boat and walked across the beautiful green lawn that was covered with poop, feathers, blood, and dead geese.

The owner had an irrigation system and took much pride in growing his Kentucky Bluegrass lawn. But the green lawn was like a magnet to the goose families living in the area. They would eat the grass then leave droppings all over the man's property, boat, and dock. Once I secured the shotgun and interviewed the shooter, I began collecting dead baby geese. Unable to fly, the geese were very easy prey for the shotgun-wielding men. He shot 19 of them.

Although killing the young 19 half-grown Canada geese out of goose season was a dumb thing, I still had a little compassion for the man due to the mess he had to contend with from the geese.

I still arrested him, though. Understanding why he killed the geese, and knowing the motivation that he had when shooting the geese, led me to contact the judge to inform him of the totality of the situation. On the one hand, the landowner was a cruel, cold-hearted poacher who killed defenseless baby geese. On the other hand, he was an irate homeowner who had had enough of the messy intruders. Definitely another case of mixed emotions.

Old School Supervisor

T he "good old days" are times that happened not that long ago. There was a great era in law enforcement where officers were trusted and respected by most people. This era took place before several negative factors and an anti-police sentiment, and police over-scrutiny. In the good old days, an officer was respected and entrusted to make proper decisions and be honest and trustworthy. Somehow, due to only a few bad apples, the pendulum has swung so far against the police community that we think nothing of the implementation and use of body cams, GPS tracking devices, and dashcams. These devices are often used to prove an officer's innocence and to verify officer's accounts of situations.

Philosophically speaking, I believe that almost all police officers are good, honest, trustworthy people. I know from being a Background Investigation Officer for the State of Michigan for many years that only the best officer candidates are advanced in the hiring process. We thoroughly check applicants' histories and behavior patterns to ensure we are only placing uniforms on the best citizens. We talk to old friends, school teachers, and employers of potential officers before we proceed with oral interviews and psychological testing of the applicants. Contrary to news and television reports, only those candidates with the utmost integrity, honesty, and impeccable backgrounds become officers.

Because almost all police officers are honest and trustworthy, they should be treated accordingly by their department. If a sergeant, lieutenant or police chief trusts and believes in an officer's integrity, then it is much easier to defend that officer against false accusations.

False accusations against police officers seem to be quite common nowadays. It seemed uncommon to be falsely accused of wrongdoing in the good old days. But one time a subject called a false complaint in on me back then about an incident that happened one afternoon when I was on patrol. A white van crossed the center line on a two-lane road and almost hit my patrol car head on. I swerved and then did a u-turn, and then caught up to the van. I hit my flashers, and then the driver pulled into the parking lot of a local bar and restaurant called the Dorsey House.

When the van stopped, I walked up toward the driver's door at which time the drunk driver got out. I said, "Oh, how's it going today?" and "please have a seat back in your van."

The driver looked at me and kept walking toward me. I said, "Oh, you don't have any knives or guns on you, do you?" The driver immediately pulled a six-inch buck knife out of his pocket and he locked the blade in the open position and continued walking at me. Oh great. Should I shoot him or just kick his butt, I thought. The subject was now almost too close to me for me to draw my gun and kill him, so I did the next best thing. Stupidly, I grabbed the subject's arm and roughly threw him to the ground. Knife still in hand, the subject, now face down,) was laying on his folded arms and would not comply with my orders to put his hands behind his back. I was forced to manhandle the knife wielding subject and was able to bring his hands behind his back and place him in handcuffs! Several bar patrons and citizens gathered around me as I made my arrest. Anyway, I arrested the man for the knife incident and drunk driving and then continued working.

The next day one of the onlookers at the bar parking lot called my lieutenant Jim Gilhart to complain about how violently I handled the situation. The bad witness told lieutenant Gilhart that I had thrown the subject 30 feet through the air. Now, remember this was in the "good old days" when this happened. If it were nowadays, there would be a formal complaint, a Department of Justice investigation, and a suspension upon hearing the complaint. But because of the era, there was a different outcome. My lieutenant asked the witness again, how far the officer threw the subject. Again, the caller said 30 feet through the air. Lieutenant Gilhart then said "bull****", you are a liar, even though John is strong, he nor anybody else could throw a man 30 feet through the air. So as far as I am concerned since you lied about the throwing distance, everything you have to say is also a lie, so goodbye!." Wow. We had a supervisor who believed in us and who would defend us. Here was a situation where I was justified to use deadly force, but instead, went hands on to neutralize the assailant. No one got hurt, the subject went to jail, and I safely made it home later that day.

I'm afraid that in many current situations, officers are tentative and are always worried about discipline to the point where officer safety could be jeopardized. If an officer hesitates when dealing with a dangerous situation due to fear of discipline or is afraid of public outcry, he or she could be placing themselves in harm's way. I hope the good old days return, where the "good guys" are the police and we place our trust and faith back in our law enforcement community!

Convicted Terrorist Caught Poaching

L aw enforcement jobs can be very dangerous at times. Dealing with armed criminals adds to the degree of danger. Dealing with a convicted terrorist with a .243 centerfire rifle (which incidentally would penetrate right through most police bullet-proof vests) adds even more to the danger scale. This dangerous situation happened one deer season.

Yet another deer season patrol turned into a major ordeal. While heading east on a dead end gravel road, I could see a white SUV parked at the end. When I got closer, I saw someone sitting in the vehicle. The passenger side window was rolled down. As I approached the subject, I noticed a six-point buck inside the back of the vehicle. I made small talk for a while, then asked the big question, who shot the deer? "Oh, I did," the subject said. I could see a tag attached to the small buck's antlers, so I acted like there were no violations. Just for kicks, I said, "Can I check your gun that is right next to you to make sure that it is not loaded?" His window was rolled down which made me wonder if possibly his gun could have been loaded. The 12-gauge shotgun was not loaded even though the case was totally unzipped. Then I saw another gun case under the 12-gauge gun case. I grabbed it, but it was empty. "That's my dad's case," the subject stated. He said his dad was out hunting. Sounds reasonable, I thought to myself until I saw the green and yellow Remington brand trademark box of .243 ammo next to the empty gun case. I became more suspicious because centerfire rifles were not allowed for deer hunting in this part of Michigan.

I began looking closer at the vehicle and its contents. Upon studying the kill tag on the deer, I realized that it was not validated. I ran the license number on the kill tag through our DNR dispatch center, and it did come back to the subject's father. The tag did not belong to the 30-year-old subject sitting in the vehicle who claimed that he had shot the deer. Now, I became more suspicious because of the deer, the empty case, and the rifle ammo. Officers intuition led me to do a complete check of the individual's drivers license printed on the kill tag. I radioed in to check on the owner of the tag. The radio traffic sounded like this:

"Station 20 from 9-134." "Go ahead 9-134." "Station 20, can you run a driver's license number for me?" After giving my dispatcher the driver's license number, the radio traffic went like this: "9-134 your subject comes back with an officer safety caution for several felonies and weapons charges."

I said, "OK station 20, can you run a criminal history check on the subject?" Then I heard, "Station 20 to 9-134, your subject is a convicted terrorist who also has multiple charges of resisting arrest, fleeing police, and several weapons charges." "OK, 9-134 clear. Wait. Did you say convicted terrorist, station 20?" "That's affirmative."

The long list of felonies prohibited the suspect from even owning or possessing a firearm. Now is when I went into enhanced battle mode and went searching for the convicted felon. Or was I searching for a terrorist? Or was I searching for a deer poacher? I was searching for all three, all wrapped up into one person wandering around with a high power rifle. I did request assistance, and two St. Clair County Sheriff Department deputies did respond to help me attempt to locate the felon. After an unsuccessful search for the suspect, I thanked the deputies and told them that I would call for help once I found the poacher. The deputies then left the area.

I searched for a couple of hours; I even tried to trick him into coming out of the woods by leaving the scene temporarily. But he was nowhere to be found. Right around dusk, I was slowly walking through an abandoned farmyard, checking in tall grass and around old rusty farm implements and junk piles. I came around the back of a crumbling outbuilding, and something caught my attention only 15 feet away in the brush. It was my felon, lying there in full camouflage and holding a loaded scoped rifle! Don't move, police, conservation officer don't move, were among some of the choice words I used as I aimed my Springfield .308 M1A rifle at the suspect. I pounced on the poacher and placed him in handcuffs. He did not resist me, he never even shot at me. I'm sure he could have shot me as I searched for him but for some reason, he never pulled the trigger. I called dispatch and advised them that I found my prize. I arrested him for felony firearms possession, taking a deer illegally, and hunting without orange clothing among other charges.

Conservation officers and police officers never know what dangerous situation they might be facing while conducting their law enforcement duties. By digging a little deeper, searching more vigorously, and questioning a bit more, I figured out the type of violation and what type of criminal I was dealing with. I also was able to effect a very good arrest and through tactical and safe searching and with a little luck, I lived to write about it.

Flight, Fight, or Both

People always say a conservation officer's job is the most dangerous police job because everyone we come into contact with is armed during hunting season. Most of the time, they are wrong. We just deal with a bunch of great people who have guns. But once in awhile the people with the guns are not so great. Most conservation officers work alone, and backup officers could be as far as an hour away, which only adds to the potential danger of the job.

The other area of concern is when poachers or criminals either choose the "flight" or "fight" option upon contact with an officer. Most people do neither, they don't run and they don't fight. There are, however, poachers who are non-cooperative criminals, and often choose the flight option over the fight option. They flee on foot, in cars, boats, ORV's, motorcycles, and snowmobiles. It's fun trying to outthink, outrun, outdrive, and outlast those in the "flight" group. Then there is the small percentage of poachers or criminals that would rather fight than flee. Since almost all of our contacts with hunters involve the hunter being armed, these people who stand and fight become very dangerous. They are armed and do not give up right away, and they do not flee. This story involves a subject that chose both the flight and fight options.

Late bow season was upon us again when I got a call about someone trespassing and shooting on the Detroit Edison private property adjacent to the sandy shores of Lake Huron.

The Edison's 400-acre parcel was very well posted with no hunting or trespassing signs. Large blue and white signs were posted around its perimeter, leaving no room for error for intruders. I checked the area several times and found no signs of trespassing.

Then one morning, I decided to go for a walk to look for poachers and trespassers. As I walked the beautiful land, I jumped a couple of deer, and also spotted a flock of turkeys. Then, I caught movement from a couple hundred yards away. I could barely make out the silhouette of a subject dressed in full camo sneaking around in the woods. I got a little closer and I could see that he had a scoped gun. I tried to get even closer, but the suspect saw me and began running. I yelled, "Stop, conservation officer! Stop, police," several times as I chased after the poacher. He had a considerable lead.

I called dispatch and advised them that I was chasing a man with a gun and asked for backup. The suspect was running south toward Fischer Road. As I pursued the suspect, I kept yelling, "Stop, police, stop," but the chase continued. I began gaining on the fleeing trespasser. Soon, I saw him run around the corner of a red pole barn that was located behind a residence.

Still running, when I came around the corner of the barn, I was met face to face by the suspect. He was holding his gun and staring at me at a dangerously close distance of only 20 feet away. I was loudly yelling, "Drop your gun, police, drop your gun." Unbeknownst to me, a homeowner heard me yelling and looked out his window and then called 9-1-1. The caller advised dispatch that a man was pointing his rifle at a police officer. This information added even more urgency to my request for assistance.

Critical incidents and shooting incidents unfold so fast. But the elements involved in this incident seemed to present themselves in a deliberate, methodical method. Man in camo, scoped gun, close distance, no cover, no backup, I continued yelling, "Drop your gun," as I began pulling my trigger back to shoot the poacher. Not dropping his gun forced me several times during the standoff to pull the trigger on my .40 caliber Sig Sauer. I would pull the trigger, and then right before my gun would have gone off, I would notice that his muzzle was not **directly** pointed at my body.

Eventually, the suspect threw his gun down and just stood there challenging me. I ordered the suspect to the ground to facilitate placing him in handcuffs. But when I went to handcuff him, he decided to fight with me. After fighting him for a while, I placed the idiot in handcuffs. I could hear the police car sirens in the distance as they approached my location. Then, I got another surprise, the handcuffed suspect came at me to fight again. He lost again. St. Clair County Sheriff Deputies and Sanilac County Sheriff Deputies all soon arrived and helped me with evidence, statements, and lodging the suspect in jail. Several serious charges were filed against the suspect.

The suspect asked for a jury trial, only one of two that I ever had. In court, he told the jury that during our standoff, "The officer used some kind of crazy martial arts take down," and that, "I never saw anything like it before." I thought to myself that if he did not want to see it again, don't be a felon with a gun, don't go poaching, and don't run from me and don't fight with me. He was convicted of being a felon in possession of a firearm, of poaching and resisting and obstruction of an officer along with many other crimes. After he was released from prison, I never had a negative experience with this suspect again. Matter of fact, he stopped me one day to apologize for his actions and for lying at his trial. I accepted his apology but then I advised the poacher to stay clear of me. I smiled as I told him that I was neither afraid of him nor intimidated by him. I was civil to him but I let him know that he would lose again if he poached or resisted my arrest again.

Handgun in Van

One night while I was sneaking around on the back roads hunting for deer poachers, I had another dangerous encounter. St. Clair County Sheriff Department dispatcher Mark Johnson was working with me. While driving slow and scanning the horizon for spotlights, we spotted a vehicle parked on the road without lights on just ahead of us. Figuring the van was broken down or possibly the owner was raccoon hunting, we walked up to check it out.

As I looked into the side rear window, I saw a man lying down looking at me, and he had a blued steel pistol next to his hand. "Don't move," I yelled as I drew my gun. "Don't move, don't touch the gun," I said over and over. "Keep your hands up," I yelled. I called for a backup car. In the meantime, I told Mark to get my shotgun out and use it only if I got shot while I was trying to get the suspect out.

The suspect just stared at me, the handgun only inches away from his hand. At this point, I did not know what was wrong with him or if the man had any other guns with him, so this scene was very unsecured. The man in the van had a blank look on his face, and he refused my orders to raise his hands and to come out of the van. I had a dilemma; I could not secure the gun without climbing all the way through the van. It was kind of a standoff. When my backup officer, Scott Sabata from Yale Police Department arrived, we devised a plan.

Scott and Mark would cover me, and I would meet the gun possessing man in his van. I would grab his gun and bring him out. Kind of a gutsy plan, but all went well. I climbed into the old conversion style van and cautiously approached the subject. The subject still showed no emotion as I grabbed the loaded gun, then him. I helped him from the inside of his van, and we placed the suspect in custody. I called dispatch to check to see if the gun was stolen. Upon checking the serial numbers on the gun, the dispatcher advised me that the gun had never been registered. The subject had no explanation for what he was doing or why he had the handgun. He still had a blank look on his face, so I decided to get his attention to let him know the severity of the situation. I decided to mess with him.

After all, the suspect was acting like it was no big deal to have the illegal handgun, and that it was just fine not to cooperate with the police. I asked the man, "Have you ever been in Tennessee?" I then told him that the computer check of the gun showed that the gun was used in a murder in Tennessee. "What, I didn't do it," he denied killing anyone, over and over. The subject finally showed some emotion. Visibly shaken and concerned that he was going to get charged with a murder finally made him understand the severity of the situation. After letting him panic for quite a while, I told him the truth and arrested him. Sometimes we never find out what people are really doing but I was happy to get an illegal handgun away from a very strange individual.

How Did that Sturgeon Get In My Boat

How difficult is it to catch a serious poacher? It is so hard to be in the right place at the right time and then make all the right moves and actions to arrest a real poacher. For example, let's look at how nearly impossible it was to catch one particular sturgeon poacher.

First of all, I needed to be working on that exact night. This means that I could not have had the day off, or had training or a meeting, or any other assigned tasks. I had to be at the exact location of the poachers' activities and not be one mile or ten or sixty miles away watching someone else. I needed to zero in on this one particular boat, and I needed to have some reason or probable cause to stop the boat. I needed to gently intrude into their area of privacy and personal belongings. The fourth amendment applies (where any governmental intrusion into an area of privacy requires a search warrant or use of one of the ten exceptions such as a "consent search").

Once I was legally on the suspects' boat, I needed to use my experience and expertise (or luck) to find anything illegal.

So you see, with all of the obstacles, obstructions, pitfalls and all that could go wrong, the chances of a serious poacher getting caught are very slim (there is probably less than a 1% chance of getting caught).

So I went on patrol hoping to beat the odds as I hunted for fish poachers. Almost everyone either fishes, eats fish, or enjoys seeing fish here in Michigan. Fish generate millions of dollars of revenue each year. In 2011, $2.4 billion dollars was spent on fishing and fishing equipment. Part of a Michigan Conservation Officer's job is to protect the different fish species. Ensuring future fish populations is accomplished through patrolling for violations of seasons, methods, licensing, and "catch limits" placed on certain species.

So while I was out one night in May, I checked along the St. Clair River searching for fish poachers. The vast majority of fishermen obey the fishing laws. However, as in any group, there are always a few who cheat (or get greedy) and catch and keep more than the legal limit of fish. After checking several anglers, I soon found out that the fish were biting. Almost all of the fishermen caught their limit of walleye and then headed home to clean fish and go to bed.

I watched guys in a few boats catching fish at 1:00 a.m., then 2:00 a.m., and by 4:00 a.m. I had a hunch that some of the fishermen may be keeping more than the legal limit of walleyes. Now at 5:00 a.m., I zeroed in on one particular boat and stopped it. Knowing the limit of fish was six fish per person per day, I would always ask in an unassuming way, "How are you guys doing tonight?" Small talk led to the big question, "How did you guys do tonight?" There were three men aboard the boat. One stated they caught 14 walleye, the second said they caught 18 walleye, and the third said, "We did pretty good, maybe 15." Great news to a Michigan Conservation Officer who had worked all night, someone was lying or just could not count. I asked if I could see their fish and they said yes. I gently but confidently climbed into the now suspects' boat just to see their fish. Making small talk and checking coolers, I counted fish, and continued looking and counted more fish. When the total count exceeded more than their legal 18 fish limit, I began looking even harder for more hidden fish. Bingo, I found more walleyes hidden under some life jackets.

Now with a concrete violation in hand and three suspects milling around me in their 19-foot fiberglass boat, I was even more determined to find more fish. I lifted up one of the vinyl seats and the entire seat lifted up. As I was looking for more 18 inch long walleyes, I got a huge surprise. Right in front of me, hidden under the seats was a five foot long sturgeon! Sturgeon are highly protected by season and catch limits, and the legal season was not even open for another month.

Adrenaline flowing and trying not to smile with pride from finding the hidden illegal fish, I asked the poachers the next big question, who caught this big sturgeon? The men all told me that they "DID NOT KNOW HOW THE FISH GOT INTO THEIR BOAT"! Over and over again they lied to me about not knowing how the fish got into their boat. The fish must have lifted up the seats and hid so well. I advised the three liars that they were all under arrest for possession of an over limit of walleyes and possession of an illegal sturgeon. Finally, one of the subjects manned up and admitted to catching and hiding the sturgeon.

I issued tickets to the three men and seized all of their fish, and being a little tired, went home and went to bed. I was smiling and content from the great cases that I had made, I fell asleep at about 7:00 a.m.

My phone rang at 8:00 a.m. After one hour of sleep, I was greeted with, "This is the lieutenant from the Special Operations Unit of the Michigan State Police." The lieutenant advised me that their computer picked up on my incident from a couple of hours earlier because I had checked my three suspects for warrants. Then the state police lieutenant told me that the three poachers were being watched and were going to be arrested the next day for a major crime spree. The three men each owned party stores and were buying stolen items from street criminals and selling them by the thousands in their stores. I was shocked to learn that the three men were all carrying loaded .9 mm pistols with them while I searched their boat.

I guess they could have taken me out at any time, but I can't help but wonder if my calm and friendly demeanor may have played a role in the situation not escalating.

All three men were arrested the next day, and all sent to federal prison. And me, I'm still here trying to protect our valuable fish resource.

Never Back Down

I was hired as a Michigan Conservation Officer on September 5th, 1985. After years without hiring any new officers, the DNR Law Division hired five new officers. Along with my appointment, the DNR also hired Ron Pinson, Jane Dunn, Pat Blair, and Linda Gallagher. The good news for Michigan was that five new officers were joining the force to help protect our natural resources. The bad news was that after years without hiring, the DNR was a little slow in the training process.

One of my future partners, Ron Pinson, was the only one of us five new hired officers who was already a certified officer! Ron transferred from the Michigan State Police, so he was ready to work. The rest of us new officers were sent to work before we even attended a police academy. We were all put on a training schedule which had us riding with senior officers around the state. We would show up in uniform, with a marked patrol car, and work with the veteran officer for two weeks at a time. Lt. Roger Wood orchestrated all of our days, times, and locations. Through his work, everything went smooth. We would just show up to different areas and frankly, just go to work. We got free hotel rooms, free meals, and were getting paid conservation officer wages. It was like being on a paid one year vacation while performing an interesting job. No wonder I enjoyed my career so much, with a start like that, who wouldn't?

Anyway, as I bounced from district to district, I got to meet and work with some exceptional officers. I got to work with legendary officers like Mitch Babcock, Charlie Turk, Ron McCarty, John Casto, Mike Rademacher, Bob Clark, Bob Snider, Tim Cohany, Walt Mikula, Steve McLurg, Henry Miazga, Lynn Ward, Gary Turnquist, and Jim Gallie to name a few. What a way to learn people skills and learn about resource issues.

On several of my two-week stints working western Michigan, I had the privilege of working with Mitch Babcock, Charlie Turk, and Ron McCarty.

One day while working near White Cloud, Michigan, we set out searching for salmon poachers. Charlie, Ron, Mitch and I searched different areas along the Pere Marquette River. The river was full of spawning salmon. Monster trophy fish were lined up on the shallow gravel shoals in the clear waters.

Mitch sent me north along the river and off I went, without a radio or partner. I walked and walked, and after about one mile, I heard voices ahead of me and snuck up on two salmon snaggers. The poachers were using lead weighted (M-60) treble hooks. The men had seven large salmon on a stringer in front of them; then I watched one of them snag a large female salmon. The M-60 was hooked in the side, and after reeling in the hooked fish, the subject put it on the stringer. I stepped out of my hiding spot and announced my presence.

I told the poachers that they were going to get tickets for snagging. Then I advised them that I would carry all of their fishing gear and fishing rods. Knowing that we had a long walk back to the patrol car, I instructed the snaggers to drag the illegal fish all the way back to their waiting tickets (since I had no ticket book). The subjects began dragging the load of fish behind them. About halfway back to the car, the subjects stopped, and one of them yelled to me, "beep you! We're not dragging the fish anymore, if you want the fish for evidence, then you drag them! We're not going with you anymore either!"

I had a huge decision to make. Was I going to be a man or a mouse? The violators were refusing to go with me and were refusing the drag the illegal fish. I threw down their fishing rods and tackle, and I abruptly stated, "Then let's do this the old fashioned way. If you two think you can win in a fight against me, then come on and try it." Then I said, "The losers have to drag the fish." The two stunned poachers looked up at me, thought about the options, then reached down and picked up the rope and said, "Fine, we'll pull the fish the rest of the way." All went well when we finally reached the waiting patrol car. Mitch wrote them tickets for the illegal fishing, and he seized their fish. What an interesting situation to be thrown into so early in my career. What was I supposed to do, just let them intimidate me and refuse to cooperate? I don't think so.

Thrill Killers

These thrill killers poached between 60 and 100 of our deer. It took several months and hundreds of hours of hard work to make this case. But the time and work was very well worth it. This case ranks near the top as one of the biggest deer poaching cases ever made in Michigan by a single officer. This case includes many different criminal elements. Killing deer out of season, killing deer at night with the aid of a spotlight, shooting from vehicles, wanton waste of game animals, trespassing, and shooting cats and farm animals are some of the crimes committed. There was a lot of public sentiment, and almost a lynch mob mentality that spread around the county when I caught these poachers. And for good reason.

The case all began when I noticed a dead deer lying in a cut bean field one day in early November. The deer had been shot in the neck with a small-caliber rifle. "Poacher alert," I thought as I patrolled the area. The following week in the same area, I received a call about a dark truck with someone shining from the truck. The caller said that he heard a gunshot and then saw the truck speed away. I responded to the location and found a freshly killed doe with a small caliber bullet hole in the neck. The caller told me that the truck was dark and likely a Dodge. The next night I found three dead deer dumped in a ditch, and all had small caliber bullet holes in them. Five deer, all shot with a small caliber rifle, made me sick. I searched the wound channels on the deer and soon found the rifle bullets. The bullets were most likely .17 caliber.

Similar to the police detective shows where they piece together several murders to begin a serial murder case, I began working on my serial poaching case. Night after night I would patrol, searching for the mystery pickup truck. I found three more gun shot deer in the general vicinity. I plotted the location of the poached deer on a county map. I collected bullet fragments and blood samples from the deer and continued patrolling. The next piece of the puzzle came from a subject who was one of my students that I had had in my conservation law enforcement class that I taught at the local college. He told me that he saw a black Dodge pickup truck speed away from where they had shot at a deer while they were shining one night near his home. I began crisscrossing the 20-mile area searching for the suspects' black Dodge truck. Day after day, night after night I patrolled, and then I got yet another bit of information. This information came from a girl who stated that her friends were bragging that they had shot 25 deer already while using a rifle and a spotlight. A serial poaching case. Unfortunately, the girl only knew the first names of the poachers, but she did know that they drove a black truck and that they did live in the Emmett area. The next piece of the puzzle came from a subject I had previously arrested for shining and shooting a deer. The past customer was very polite and remorseful over his incident and thanked me for treating him fairly. He told me he heard a rumor that some kids from Emmett were killing a lot of deer using a spotlight and a .17 caliber rifle. The only thing that he knew for sure was that the subjects drove a black Dodge pickup truck and that they played a lot of hockey.

So along with patrolling day and night, I began going to hockey arenas looking for the black truck. I then contacted all the high school, pro, and travel hockey teams in the area and started quizzing them for information. Along with the patrolling and detective work, I now became a hockey fan. I then got a call from a friend of mine who was awakened at 2:00 a.m. by three gun shots. The caller told me that he had seen a black pickup truck driving away. He quickly jumped into his truck and took off after the poachers' truck. He could not get a license plate but did tell me that the suspects' truck was indeed a black Dodge Big Horn edition pickup truck. The caller also said that the truck had a piece of yellow rope hanging down from its trailer hitch. I searched the area near the caller's home and I did locate three .17 caliber rifle casings on the road. For the next few weeks, I searched everywhere for the black Dodge Big Horn edition truck with the yellow rope hanging down from the trailer hitch. I kept collecting deer as evidence and continued searching as the puzzle started to piece together. I knew I was closing in on a black truck driven by four to six hockey players who were using a .17 caliber rifle and spotlight to kill deer. Night after night, I stayed up late searching for my poachers. Then, one Sunday afternoon in January, it happened.

I had stopped a snowmobiler and was giving the operator a verbal warning. Just then, the St. Clair County Sheriff, Tim Donnellon, pulled up next to me. The sheriff and I had a pleasant conversation about such things as our family, sports, and a little about our jobs. As we were talking, I looked up and I saw a black Dodge pickup truck coming toward me. As the truck passed by me, I noticed that it was a big horn edition and then I saw the tell-tale yellow rope hanging down from the trailer hitch.

I quickly jumped into my truck and pulled over the suspects' vehicle. As I walked up to the truck, I noticed the back seat was full of all sorts of hockey gear and hockey sticks. Bingo, I smiled and called for more backup. Once I searched the occupants, I began checking the inside of the truck. I found two boxes of .17 caliber ammunition, and then I found one uncased .17 caliber bolt action scoped rifle. Finally, the puzzle pieces were all fitting together. From the information that I had received and from all my hard work, I was sure that I had found the deer poachers. I then began interviewing the two men in the truck. First, I got written confessions from both of the young poachers in the Big Horn edition Dodge.

The author with one of 60-100 deer killed ruthlessly by poachers.

Then, I systematically tracked down the other four suspects. It took me another 11 hours to meet and interview all of the suspects. One suspect was working at a manufacturing plant, and his foreman let me walk right up to him as he worked. When the suspect's break time came, I walked the subject to my patrol truck. I had intentionally put one of the .17 caliber rifles that he had used in the front seat of my patrol truck. The gun was tagged as evidence and was laying next to the poacher in the front seat. I kept looking down at the gun while I was talking to the suspect. The poacher's eyes kept glancing down to the familiar gun sitting next to him. It was almost cheating to place the gun that he had used to illegally shoot deer next to him. But not really. After awhile, the suspect gave me a written confession as to his involvement in the deer poaching.

All told, all six poachers gave written confessions to killing between 60 and 100 deer by use of spotlights and the .17 caliber rifles. The subjects also confessed to shooting cats and other animals and were contemplating shooting a cow or even an elk at an elk enclosure. One of the subjects told me that on a few occasions, they would sit on and pretend to be "riding the bull" on injured deer that they had shot! All six subjects pleaded guilty without trials. Over $20,000 in restitution was paid to the state of Michigan for the deer killed. Two .17 caliber rifles were condemned by the court. Each subject lost his hunting privileges in Michigan (and several other cooperating states) for the following four years, and six poachers were out of business.

Moving Target Practice

Just when I thought that I had seen it all, I walked up on this situation of four guys target shooting. Target shooting is an American pastime. It's fun, period. It's relaxing. The more of us that exercise our second amendment right to own firearms, the more people target shoot. I always try to allow gun enthusiasts as many opportunities to get out and shoot as I can. My policy has always been to leave people alone when shooting unless they are shooting carelessly and endangering someone. But this group, well, it was a little hard just to leave them alone.

One hot August afternoon, I was driving on Metcalf Road just west of Lake Huron when I heard several gunshots. The bursts of shots sounded like fully automatic rifle fire. I stopped and got out of my patrol vehicle and pinpointed the location of the shots as best as I could. Once I zeroed in on the area, I realized the shooting was coming from a 10-acre parcel on the south side of the road. I began walking towards the gunfire (most people go the opposite direction of gunfire, but not me, not conservation officers). The shots came in volleys of 30 to 60 at a time. As I approached the location of the shots, I could hear yelling and laughing between volleys.

Eventually, I got close enough to see who was doing the shooting. Three males in their early twenties were shooting at a white two-door Chevy car. Not just any white car, though. You see, one of their friends was driving a large jacked up red pickup truck that had a chain hooked up to the white car. The car was upside down, and the red truck was driving around in circles real fast. Each time the white car passed the three men, they shot their assault rifles and shotguns at the completely upside down moving car. It's too bad. I do not have video or pictures of this dangerous, hilarious, and amusing sight. I walked closer to the three dummies. After each time they shot, I would get closer to them while they were reloading. Dumbfounded, I dealt with the subjects and then drove away shaking my head.

Judge Needed a Recess

In a courthouse, judges are at the top of the food chain. They are the ultimate boss of what goes on. They are respected by the police, attorneys, defendants, and the public.

Most judges earn respect from how they remain professional and almost stoic when dealing with court cases. Being firm, strict, fair, and having a no-nonsense approach seems to describe most judges.

Even though one of my great judges fit the above description of someone who commanded respect and was always fair and firm, he totally lost all composure during this particular case.

The case that I brought in front of the judge all began on a warm September day. As I was walking along the Black River, I heard a single .22 shot about a half mile away. Maybe someone shot a squirrel, I thought. About five minutes later, I heard a second .22 shot and then five minutes later, I heard another shot. Then five or six minutes later, I heard another shot. I thought that someone must be having some real good luck. But after 15 single-spaced out shots, I began walking in the direction of the shots (yes I know, we are a strange group of people, we walk toward people shooting with guns instead of going the other way). Soon I focused on an area where I thought the shots were coming from. After walking for awhile, I caught a glimpse of a subject dressed in full camouflage, and then I saw him raise his scoped .22 rifle and shoot again. I kept creeping closer to try to see what the heck the plentiful game was that he was shooting at. I had to sneak up very cautiously and quietly on the hunter because he kept looking behind him. It was obvious to me that he was doing something wrong by the number of times he looked around and by how he kept checking behind him. Then I saw the subject shoot a robin, you know, the Michigan state bird. I approached the subject as soon as he placed the bird in his backpack. "Hi," I said. "How you doing, are you having any luck?"

No was the answer. I asked, "Did you shoot anything today," and he said, "no, nothing." I told the subject that I needed to see what was inside his backpack. When I opened it, I found that it was full of robins. I advised the subject of the violation of killing nongame birds, and for hunting without hunter orange clothing. I issued him tickets and continued working.

About a month later, I had to go to court for a pretrial regarding the robin poacher. The pretrial was scheduled in front of District Court Judge John Cummings. Judge Cummings asked the robin killer if he knew that killing robins was illegal, and the man stated, "Yes." Then the judge asked him why he was killing robins. His answer was blunt and to the point, "Good to eat." Judge Cummings said, "What?" "Good to eat," was the answer again. The judge then started laughing and could not talk any longer and then recessed the court and walked into his chambers. After about five minutes, the judge came back to the bench and asked the subject again, "Why did you shoot the robins?" and the "good to eat" answer came out again. I know judges hear about everything when they have defendants in front of them. They hear the strangest cases and the most bizarre excuses, but this time, this situation must have hit his funny bone. Judge Cummings started laughing again and recessed the court for a full 10 minutes more. I went into the judge's chambers, and we both began laughing until we had tears in our eyes. The judge told me that what was so funny was the look on the poacher's face when he described the tiny tablespoon full of meat found in a robin's breast that is good to eat and worth the risk of getting caught. Finally, the judge did accept the guilty plea and then went on to hear the other cases of the day such as auto theft, larceny, drug cases, and weapons charges.

My New Poaching Law

There is a saying that "beauty is in the eye of the beholder." I think that saying applies to women all right. I think that it applies to things like cars, homes, and clothing also. But when it comes to deer, it usually does not apply. The fact is, overwhelmingly, bucks are sought after and valued more than does. Sorry, no gender disrespect intended, but bucks with large antlers are more desirable than does. And yes, all deer are trophies.

It is tough for a buck to become old enough to grow large antlers. Becoming an older trophy buck means that the buck has survived several hunting seasons, avoided car-deer accidents, and avoided predators for years. If and when a buck survives and becomes a majestic trophy, it becomes highly sought after by hunters and poachers alike. Everyone likes to shoot big bucks.

How many does do hunters take to the taxidermy shop to get mounted? How many articles in hunting magazines focus on shooting a trophy doe? Most all hunters, when given the opportunity while hunting and seeing a twelve-point buck standing next to a doe, would shoot the twelve-point buck. Realizing the value and great interest in bucks led me to try to get tougher laws to protect these bucks. For years, I tried to get more strict poaching laws enacted. "That's a great idea," "we agree," and "we will look at your ideas," was all that I heard and as far as I got. Then I devised a plan.

For a couple of years, I spoke to sportsman's clubs, quality deer management clubs, and to DNR officers at meetings. I began by saying that deer are very important to us here in Michigan. I spoke about how deer and deer hunting bring millions of dollars into our economy. Then I explained the fact that deer have been devalued over the years. I know, some of the dislike for deer is justified. Car-deer accidents and crop damage both cost millions of dollars. Injuries, deaths, costly automotive repairs and crop losses all illustrate that having too large of a deer herd has devastating negative effects.

However, due to negative publicity and some less than favorable opinions of deer, many people began thinking that deer were becoming nuisance animals similar to rats, carp, and seagulls. "Kill them all" and "there are too many deer anyway" became common phrases. But to those of us who love to see deer and hunt deer, this deer-hating attitude was not acceptable.

So, I had my work cut out for me. Some areas had too many deer. Most areas had an unbalanced herd where does made up a disproportionate number of deer in the herd. I needed to emphasize that we needed to protect the antlered deer while still controlling deer numbers in certain areas.

I would speak to the clubs and officers about the net worth of our deer herd. The net worth of our deer herd is enormous. Hunting deer provides both immense enjoyment value along with huge financial benefits. I would also expose an inequity that we had in our current law. Under the current law then, a person convicted of illegally killing a doe, or a three point buck, or a twelve-point buck would pay the exact same fine and get the exact same

The author's new poaching bill gets signed into law. Left to right, Nancy Borkovich, John Borkovich, daughter Chelsea Borkovich and Governor Rick Snyder, seated.

penalties. For example, a poacher would pay approximately $1,500 in total fines, costs, and restitution for a small doe and would pay the same $1,500 for killing a record Boone and Crockett twelve-point buck. There was not much of a deterrent to stop serious trophy poaching.

I also explained how deer ranches or enclosures would charge hunters by the size of the buck that hunters would shoot. Many ranches charge hunters $10,000 to $50,000 to shoot very large bucks. But if a poacher got caught killing a very large buck, his fines and costs would only be the standard $1,500. Again, not much of a deterrent. I knew that many large bucks were being stolen from the legal hunters.

My next step in the process was getting one of my partners, Ron Pinson, and MUCC member Jim Pryce along with Ray Peltier from Blue Water Better Bucks (QDMA) to help garner support for my plan to protect trophy deer. I began getting a lot of positive feedback and tons of encouragement. Then I contacted avid hunter and outdoorsman, Senator Phil Pavlov. Senator Pavlov was very interested in my plan. We met at the Gander Mountain store in Fort Gratiot and outlined the need for enhanced fines for those who poach trophy bucks.

The senator took all of my information and with great enthusiasm, returned to the state capital and began crafting a new law.

Several months, several phone conferences, and several trips by me to Lansing ensued. Once the bill was written, the fun began. Senator Pavlov then gained support for our new bill from other great legislators such as Senator Tom Casperson and Congresswoman Andrea LaFontaine. The bill went to all sorts of committees and sessions of Senate and Congress where I had to testify to the importance of deer and the importance of protecting antlered deer.

Ron Pinson (whose expertise was mainly in waterfowl), and devoted MUCC member Jim Pryce also came to Lansing to support our bill.

Finally, after years of public education and months and months of legal wrangling, the new law (affectionately referred to as the Borkovich/Pavlov poaching law) was signed by Governor Snyder.

The law targets serious poachers. What the law stipulates in simple form is that the bigger the buck that a poacher kills, the greater the fines are. It is a graduated scale which is meant to discourage the illegal taking of our trophy bucks. The law was not written in an attempt to target some poor guy who lost his job or was down on his luck who went out and shot a doe just to feed his family. It was written to target the most serious poachers!

The first case in which my new law was used was made by Michigan Conservation Officers Cory Foster and David Rodgers. These officers arrested a poacher who shot two bucks during the September youth hunt. The poacher first claimed that his six-year-old daughter had shot the bucks. One of the bucks was a huge trophy buck. Under the new poaching law, the poacher paid $12,000 in restitution alone, instead of the standard $1,500.

The second case where my new poaching law worked was on a case made by CO Ken Kovach. Officer Kovach arrested a subject who, contrary to Michigan law, shot three bucks during the 2014 deer season. The poacher's third buck was an 18-point buck, and he pled guilty and was fined $15,000 for the deer. That's $15,000 instead of the standard $1,500.

Similar to states like Ohio and Colorado, there will be many more enhanced fines levied on those who rob and steal trophy bucks in Michigan.

Sometimes, hunters disagree over such topics as archery hunting versus firearms hunting, crossbows versus traditional archery, and antler point restrictions versus no restrictions. However, overwhelmingly, most hunters band together in agreeing that poachers need to be stopped. My only hope here is that the heavy financial cost of illegally killing a trophy buck will be a strong enough deterrent to protect our precious and cherished trophy bucks.

Afterword

I worked as a Michigan Conservation Officer for 27 years. I was hired in 1985 and sworn in with a one-year freelance position. This allowed me to work in all areas of Michigan, from the Upper Peninsula to the southern Lower Peninsula along the Ohio state line. During this one-year tour of Michigan, I met thousands of great people and worked with dozens and dozens of outstanding officers.

My brothers Mike and Bruce were also Michigan Conservation Officers. We made Michigan history by becoming the only time in state history that three brothers served as conservation officers at the same time. We were all well respected and well known across the state of Michigan. All three of us received the highest honor given to conservation officers, the Shikar-Safari International Wildlife Officer of the Year Award during our careers. We were also selected as Michigan's Conservation Officer of the Year during our careers.

Wildlife 911 is a compilation of actual incidents that I encountered while I worked as a Michigan Conservation Officer.

Several of my supervisors over the years have told me that I gave too many warnings. It is my opinion that there is no such thing as giving too many warnings! I believe that law enforcement officers, in general, need to give more warnings. This approach would lead to better public relations. This way of working also gives officers more time and energy (and public support) for searching for and arresting serious criminals. I, for one, work under my self-imposed "excessive warning principle" and my "excessive quality arrest principle."

There is not a single story in this book that chronicles or focuses on minor violations. Albeit, there are a few funny and amazing stories mixed in. There are no stories written here about some poor guy who shot a doe just for meat to feed his family. There are no stories about good people who forgot their license or who somehow by accident broke a minor law. Each poacher written about "made the cut" due to their intentional, willful, and purposeful choice to break the law.

Conservation officers (or game wardens) have a passion for their job. They also have compassion for our sportsmen and sportswomen. Officers must have compassion, sympathy, and empathy for the old, young, disabled, and for all of the good people around us who make innocent mistakes or break one of the DNR's laws without any intent, and without purposely harming our natural resources.

Having compassion for the public is a valuable personality trait but being a compassionate, caring officer does not mean that the officer is somehow soft, weak, or easy to fool. Being able to know when and where to make an arrest while being firm and compassionate is very important.

An example of having compassion can be seen by how I viewed an old family friend. You see, my family had a cottage up north on Lake Huron as we were growing up. Our neighbor across the road became a very close and well-respected friend. The man was in his mid 80's and was a lumberjack. He worked as a logger during the logging days in Michigan that occurred between 1880 and 1900. The man even owned his own sawmill. He was a living part of Michigan history.

Anyway, our old friend felt guilty one day and confessed a story to us. He asked us not to turn him in for his wrongdoing. The lumberman friend proceeded to tell us that he had cut an apple in half and used a table sized salt shaker to put a little salt on the two apple halves. He then put the apple halves out in the cedar swamp behind his home. During deer season, the licensed hunter shot an eight-point buck which came to eat the apple. The apple incident took place during the time that baiting with salt was illegal. Not quite a heinous crime but the conscientious man felt bad for breaking the law.

The lumberman's salt violation paled in comparison to the respect that he had earned from years of hard and honest work. This man was not a criminal. His right hand was missing his thumb and ring finger. His left hand was missing his index and middle fingers. He sacrificed a lot during his lifetime of logging and tough work. He worked using those huge two-man crosscut saws (you know, with no motor). He was also very religious and a great family man.

Does putting a little salt on an apple somehow overshadow the man who definitely left a long shadow on Michigan? How does his "violation" compare to serious poaching?

Yes, I felt compassion for this old lumberman, long before I became an officer. This compassion and respect resonates in the incidents that I wrote about in this book.

As outrageous as some of the stories seem, they all happened. Readers of this book will feel as if they are participating in a "ride along" with me as we navigate through many dangerous and interesting wildlife and natural resource encounters. So, get into my patrol truck, put your seatbelt on, and get ready to experience many amazing, interesting, amusing, maddening, and unbelievable incidents. So, let's check into service, "9-134 and his readers are in service!".

About the Author

The love and admiration of nature is what drew John Borkovich to this profession. As John became more and more interested with the natural resources around him, he realized that he wanted and needed to dedicate himself not only to enjoying and respecting our wildlife, but also to protecting our fish, game, and natural resources.

John graduated with honors in 1980 from Michigan State University with a bachelor's degree. John was hired as a Michigan Conservation Officer in 1985 and was given a one year freelance assignment to work around the state of Michigan.

He was part of the DNR Firearms Transition Team, and was also a firearms instructor. He was a Field Training Officer for recruit conservation officers, and was an instructor at the Conservation Officer Police Academy held at the Michigan State Police headquarters in Lansing. John received many safe driving awards, and received recognition for his "Fit for Duty" performances.

John was an adjunct professor at St. Clair County Community College in the criminal justice department. He developed the curriculum for two separate courses at the college and taught the Conservation Law Enforcement and Environmental Law Enforcement classes.

He has received many awards and accommodations: The Shikar Safari International Wildlife Officer of the Year Award (incidentally, John's brothers Mike and Bruce also were selected to receive this award during their careers). National Wildlife Turkey Federation Michigan Officer of the Year. John received lifesaving awards, and has been recognized several times by St. Clair County Sheriff Department and the Michigan State Police for his work.

John currently works as a police officer for the city of Yale and Lexington Police Departments.